SOCIAL EXCELLENCE: WE DARE YOU

SOCIAL EXCELLENCE: WE DARE YOU

BY
MATTHEW G. MATTSON
JESSICA GENDRON WILLIAMS
JOSH ORENDI

A product of Phired Up Productions, LLC

Created and published by
Phired Up Productions, LLC
484 E. Carmel Dr. #335
Carmel, IN 46032

ISBN: 978-1-257-11051-3

Mattson, Matthew G, Gendron Williams, Jessica, Orendi, Josh

    Social Excellence: We Dare You / by Matthew Mattson,
    Mattson, Jessica Gendron Williams, Josh Orendi

Printed in the United States of America

First Edition

http://www.PhiredUp.com

This book is dedicated to...

STRANGERS

(but they won't be strangers for long)

TABLE OF CONTENTS

SOCIAL EXCELLENCE

WE DARE YOU

THE WORLD WOULD BE BETTER IF...

"The world would be better if..." That statement, when spoken within small groups of thoughtful, action-oriented people, has sparked revolutions, incited rebellions, provoked uprisings, and birthed the movements that have shaped our society. That's how we'd like to start off our conversation with you.

The world would be better if we were all more social, more excellent, more Socially Excellent.

The world would be better if people engaged with one another more often.

The world would be better if people were more skilled at the art of human connection.

The world would be better if we listened to the passion and enthusiasm others have about the things that are important to them.

The world would be better if we shook more hands, smiled at strangers more often, and occasionally surprised passersby with a high-five.

The world would be better if we had more powerful conversations.

The world would be better if more people participated in communities and organizations.

The world would be better if our interactions with one another were more human and less digital.

The world would be better if we were more genuine, more below-the-surface, and more real with each other.

The world would be better if we asked better questions.

3

The world would be better if we could convince more people that they have the potential to change the world.

The world would be better if more people knew how to involve others in their cause.

The world would be better if we chose to have this conversation more often—and then did something about it.

The world would be better if...

(PLEASE)

You'll soon learn that this book is not best experienced sitting by yourself. In fact, reading it alone is the antithesis of our point. We suggest reading it in a very public place and lifting your eyes from the page often to observe the people all around. This book is, after all, about being *social*.

Before you read any further, we recommend you pause to consider the challenge of being more social, take it seriously, and confidently decide to proceed. The book will reveal what it means to be more social, but it is important to begin by making a personal commitment to boldly consider this simple challenge that follows.

WE DARE YOU

The Five-Minute Challenge: Be social. Right now. Whatever that means to you. Be social. Just do it. You can't get this wrong. Just be social for five minutes before you read anything else in this book. Even just a little bit social. WE DARE YOU.

That was the first of many dares you'll be offered. How'd you do?

To be completely transparent, we want you, the reader, to start by experiencing, feeling, and living in the sensation of truly being social. Don't just think about it—do it. What you choose to do with that dare—and other dares that follow—will establish the baseline for your "social self." From there, we'll work toward excellence together.

Note from the Authors

Thanks for choosing to be the person who reads our book. Before you go too far, you should know something—we're not perfect. Not even close.

We admit we don't always live up to the philosophy and values of Social Excellence outlined in this book. Yes, we admit it. We're not always these things... but we always try to be.

We sometimes stumble. We're sometimes awkward. We sometimes embarrass ourselves in public. We forget names. We let fear get the best of us. We put our foot in our mouth. We get laughed at. We sometimes choose shyness over boldness. We sometimes stay closed off. We are a work in progress. But we try—every day. We often fail, but we fail *forward*, constantly learning and challenging ourselves further each day.

This philosophy—this lifestyle—called Social Excellence that we're sharing with you, is something we strive for each and every day and we hope you will, too. Once you do, you'll experience this incredibly empowering life change. You'll realize that you can change the world. Let us say that again...

You can change the world.

The power to change the world in a positive way lies in your ability and willingness to connect with others, gather them together around a cause that is meaningful to you, and rally that organized group of people—that organization—to make a dent in this world.

Maybe we should pause for a second before diving too deeply into changing the world. Let's take a moment to tell you a little about who we are and how we've used Social Excellence to change our world.

A few years back, around 2002, two typical, broke, clueless, twenty-four-year-old guys happened to know each other pretty well. They had just spent a year or so working together for their college fraternity's national headquarters. These two buddies had just spent their first post-university jobs accidentally learning about the world by traveling to colleges across North America and talking to college men about living a values-centered life, re-cruiting high quality members, and leading with integrity. It was a weird job, but one that proved to teach some powerful lessons.

At this point, Matt was living in a sleepy suburb of Chicago and working his new job as a college admissions counselor. About 200 miles south, Josh was in Indianapolis, trying to figure out the world of sales while working for one of the major rental car chains and experimenting with a network marketing business on the side.

These two guys both got an idea that grew out of long, philosophical phone conversations, a few late-night e-mail rants, and each reading a lot of books about business development, networking, people skills, Winning Friends and Influencing People, and the like. That idea was pretty simple.

Almost everyone has a passionate cause they care deeply about. A lot of those people gather together in small groups to impact those causes. If those small, cause-oriented groups had more of the right people, they could make a bigger impact on the world. *Why don't we help those small groups gather more people together around their cause? That could be our way to change the world!*

And thus was born the idea for the company now known as Phired Up Productions. Soon thereafter, Josh and Matt realized they weren't quite as smart as they'd been led to believe by their own young egos. They wised up. They were introduced to Jessica through a mutual friend and colleague. Jessica was this bold, social, smart, and creative woman who just exuded excellence. They clicked immediately. Thank goodness she joined the team.

Since then, Matt, Josh, and Jessica have been shaking hands, having con-versations, building relationships, collaborating with as many people as possible to help others' dreams become a reality, and building not only a company (Phired Up), but a movement. Hundreds of thousands of people have joined that movement by learning Phired Up's philosophies of Social Excellence, Dynamic Recruitment, and the power of the moment when people and purpose collide (organizations).

Telling this story is not a shameless act of self-promotion—we share this story to illustrate that Social Excellence, as you'll learn about it within these pages, works. It has helped us build our dreams, create careers that matter, and change the world for the better.

Social Excellence has helped us experience career fulfillment that we never imagined. Social Excellence has connected us in meaningful ways to high profile people we admire. Social Excellence has helped us share our products and services with a wide audience. Most importantly, Social Excellence has helped us help other people find fulfillment, build successful organizations, and change the world.

We're doing it, this Social Excellence thing. We screw up sometimes, but we're okay with that. Because we know, if we keep trying—if we get past the awkward moments, the stumbles, the gaffes, the moments of apathy—if we continually improve our own social practices, the end goal is worth it. We will have lived a life that has mattered. We will have made a meaningful, significant, positive impact on our society. We will have changed the world.

So try it. Just try it. Experiment with Social Excellence. Find ways to push yourself to be the things described in this book. Challenge yourself to test these concepts in your real life. You'll discover that just choosing to *try* some of these concepts here and there will make your days a little brighter, your life a little more enjoyable, and your organization, workplace, or community—however you decide to utilize your Social Excellence in a group environment—a lot more successful.

When we chose to adopt this lifestyle called Social Excellence, we realized our days were filled with more conversations. We realized we had more phone numbers in our contact list and it was possible to have a real relationship with most of our Facebook friends. We realized we were learning more about the world each day, and our organizations and business ventures were more effective. We realized our relationships were deeper and our lives were more meaningful. We realized our impact on the world was multiplying.

Again, we don't always get it right, but through continuously striving to adopt these principles in our life, we grow, learn, and improve.

Thank you for choosing to do the same along with us. We can't wait to meet you, shake your hand, learn from you, and make the world a better place together.

Enjoy.

How to Use This Book

Social Excellence: We Dare You is a book that is meant to be written in, wrestled with, flipped through, scribbled on, torn apart, given away, and most importantly, discussed with others.

You can't learn to be Socially Excellent by yourself.

Throughout the book, you will encounter some "Social Dares." These dares will challenge you to take what you've read and discuss or experiment with someone in the real world—ideally, with a stranger. That's right. This book actually teaches you how to connect with others, make more friends, and widen your circle of influence. And if you *fully* utilize the book, it will serve as a practical tool in helping you do it.

> "Pardon me. I'm reading this book about something called *Social Excellence* and it dared me to talk with you. Can I ask you a question?"

That phrase will become one of the most useful tools this book has to offer. The physical book you're reading, or the digital readout of it on your screen for you techno-readers, is built to serve as a door-opener, a conversation-starter, and an ice-breaker.

Will you *use* this book or just read it? Will you engage in the activities so you can engage with others? Will you learn about being social, or learn socially about being excellent? It's up to you.

We dare you.

By the way, this seems like a good time to point out that you'll want to have something to write with as you read: a pencil, pen, highlighter, crayon, stone & chisel, whatever. There are going to be lots of opportunities to circle and underline things, reflect through writing, scribble, draw pictures, sketch out a plan to change the world, draw smiley faces, and that kind of stuff. So grab something to write with. Go ahead. Do it right now. We dare you.

What this Book Is (and Isn't)

This book is about the spirit and philosophy of Social Excellence.

It isn't a complete tome on all the tactics, techniques, practices, tricks, strategies, or skills you'll need to master to reach the highest levels of Social Excellence. Nor is this book filled with social science, sociology, or modern anthropology. We have been inspired by countless authors who have contributed volumes to the subject of Social Excellence in various ways; they each provide a deeper look into individual elements of Social Excellence. We believe, however, that we have done something special by bringing lots of those thoughts (and of course some of our own) together. Our point? Read the other books we recommend—they've changed our lives and they'll change yours, too.

This book stands out because it combines the wisdom of so many others in an accessible way. It combines multiple perspectives on being "social" and turns that word into a practical recommendation for making a difference, finding fulfillment, and achieving success in life.

A list of books that have educated and inspired us related to this topic can be found at the very end of this book. We strongly recommend you enjoy and learn from these authors as well to get the true sense of what Social Excellence is about.

SOCIAL EXCELLENCE ASSESSMENT

The concept of Social Excellence will strike each reader differently. We each understand, approach, and value our social self differently. So before going much farther, let's discover your current social self.

The assessment in this section will help you to determine your current social self. Just take the assessment truthfully, and then look back at your results after you've finished reading the book. It will be eye-opening.

There is no right or wrong answer. This is a measurement tool that can provide insight into your real, current, social self—that social self will likely evolve as you experiment with the lessons of Social excellence.

So, let's start with the Five-Minute Challenge you were given just a few pages back. Did you choose to take the challenge? Did you keep reading? Did you intentionally choose to move past it because no one would know? What you chose to do when you were presented with your first of many social dares is an excellent initial test to assess your current social self. Would you score yourself pass, fail, or incomplete?

PASS	**FAIL**	**INCOMPLETE**

In the following section, please circle the number that best describes your first reaction to the statements.

Please use the key below:

1 strongly disagree   2 disagree   3 agree   4 strongly agree

When meeting a new group of people, I like to lead the conversation by sharing thoughts about myself.

1   2   3   4

The only person you can trust in this world is yourself.

1   2   3   4

It's inappropriate to ask personal questions of someone I've only known for a little while.

1   2   3   4

I'm not comfortable opening up about my personal life to strangers.

1   2   3   4

I hate to admit when I'm wrong.

1   2   3   4

I don't like it when others see my weaknesses.

1   2   3   4

I wish people would think more like me.

1   2   3   4

I'm uncomfortable with negotiation.

1   2   3   4

I prefer to communicate via text message or email over anything else.

1   2   3   4

I build relationships so I can gain from them.

1   2   3   4

I dislike social outings where I have to interact with people I don't know.

1   2   3   4

While it has value for others, this idea of changing the world isn't something that appeals to me.

1   2   3   4

I have enough friends to last me the rest of my life.

1   2   3   4

I'm annoyed by intensely passionate people.

1   2   3   4

I'm protective of my group of friends and careful who I allow in my inner circle.

1   2   3   4

I often zone out or get distracted when others are talking.

1   2   3   4

I have little to learn from people who are younger or less experienced than me.

1 2 3 4

Gathering with people to discuss causes and issues has little value for someone like me.

1 2 3 4

When I see someone being treated unjustly, I probably won't speak up.

1 2 3 4

I think community organizations are for followers/sheep/ lemmings.

1 2 3 4

I don't volunteer—I don't see the point

1 2 3 4

Most people are powerless to make a difference in the world.

1 2 3 4

Regular people have little to do with social change.

1 2 3 4

I'm uncomfortable giving a new friend a hug.

1 2 3 4

I'm uncomfortable with people who are different than me.

1   2   3   4

Add up all of your scores and put your TOTAL sum of the scores here.

_____

If you scored a **30 or below**, you're a **SOCIAL EXPERT**

Wow! You're good! Join our movement. We need people like you to not only keep being social, but to lead, guide, and mentor others as they strive for a Socially Excellent lifestyle. As an EXPERT, you'll no doubt choose to accept your role as a co-teacher of Social Excellence with us.

If you scored **31-50** you are a **SOCIAL APPRENTICE**

You have some of the skills that it takes to be Socially Excellent already. Congratulations! Your daily patterns of behavior, your personal values, and your overall mentality indicate that you're a person who understands the value of being social and acts on that value daily. No one is perfect, but you're well on your way to a Socially Excellent lifestyle... and becoming a SOCIAL EXPERT. Thanks for your commitment to discovering your best social self.

If you scored **51-79** you are a **SOCIAL STUDENT**

You may be able to execute some basic social skills, but you don't yet fully understand how being more social impacts and adds value to your life. You have some work to do to learn not only the skills and abilities of Social Excellence, but the understanding of *why* being Socially Excellent matters to you. We are so happy you have chosen to read this book. You've chosen to take the steps to learn the *how* and *why* of Social Excellence. Thanks for learning with us.

If you scored **80 or above** you are a **SOCIAL NOVICE**

Being a SOCIAL NOVICE is not bad or good. It only means you haven't yet discovered the true value that being more social will add to your life. You haven't yet mastered the skills to engage in conversation with new people and you have some work to do on your journey toward Social Excellence. Not to worry, though. That's why you're reading this book! Welcome to the Social Excellence movement. We're glad you're here. Thanks for challenging yourself in ways that may be unfamiliar and even uncomfortable. It's worth it. We promise.

To be blunt, some readers are virtual hermits, choosing to isolate themselves from humanity. Others are social superstars who live for any level of human interaction. Others are a little clueless about their social self. No matter where you fall on that continuum, this book is for you.

Anti-social behavior does not make someone a bad person. Likewise, hyper-social people are not automatically wonderful human beings. In fact, most people would be more likely to label them as "annoying." Our focus isn't about differentiating good people from bad. Rather, we are suggesting that all people can do the most good when they choose to live a life focused on bettering their own life and the lives of others.

SECTION 1

Understanding Social Excellence

1.1 THE DEFINITION

Social Excellence [n]: A state of perpetual generosity, curiosity, positivity, and openness to limitless possibility.

A desire to intentionally connect with others. The ability to engage in deep, meaningful conversation.

Acting in a responsible and respectable manner, with high expectations of others.

Being authentic and living everyday with integrity as the best version of yourself. Being confident and vulnerable.

Being fun and compassionate. Being open, kind, and bold.

The deepest level of societal participation and contribution.

Request: If you don't already have a pen, pencil, or highlighter in your hand, please get one now. Read the definition above again. Circle the words that stand out. Underline the parts that most speak to you. If a thought is lingering, take a moment to capture it in your notes right now. This will be important when we ask you to come back to the definition in a moment.

WE RECOMMEND YOU FOLD THIS CORNER SO YOU CAN EASILY COME BACK TO THE DEFINITION AS YOU PROGRESS THROUGH THE BOOK.

1.2 SOCIAL EXCELLENCE AND YOU

Reflecting on the definition from the previous page, use this space to explore your initial reaction to the definition of Social Excellence.

How well does the definition of Social Excellence define you? How does it challenge you?

How could it help you or organizations to which you belong?

What would you add to the definition of Social Excellence?

Are you ready for Social Excellence?

Now, before going further, look back at that definition and think about the people in your life. Think of someone in your life who demonstrates Social Excellence on a regular basis. Think of all your acquaintances, friends, co-workers, professors, neighbors, bosses, family members, and classmates. Think of the people in your life that are truly Socially Excellent. Point to one or two of those people in your mind's eye and focus on them. Write down their names below.

WE DARE YOU

Pick up your cell phone and scroll through the names of the relationships in your life. Write down a few names that jump off the screen at you as Socially Excellent individuals. Call and compliment them. Tell them you've noticed. Ask them if it's a conscious choice they're making. If so, ask them why and how they got so good at it. They'll be flattered. WE DARE YOU.

Write down some of the specific behaviors, traits, and characteristics you heard from the calls you just made to the Socially Excellent people in your life:

Wait! If you took the last dare, send a quick "thank you" text or e-mail to the person you called. Slip in the words "Social Excellence." As a Bonus Dare, send them a copy of this book. They deserve it.

Thinking about that person and the others on your list, you probably notice they are...

Confident amongst others, with a healthy dose of humility. Smiling more often than not. Laughing along with life. The life of the party who always knows when it's time to go home. Kind, sometimes to a fault. Great at asking questions. An expert hand-shaker. Always listening because they actually care what they might hear. Looking to help others all the time. Lacking excuses while full of the answer "yes." Polite. Comfortable with silence, but capable of traversing the awkward silences. Interested and interesting... but more interested than interesting. Fantastic at remembering names and details about each person they meet.

You might also notice they are...

Seemingly connected to everyone. Familiar with nearly everyone's topic of conversation, but honest when they have no idea what someone is talking about. Seeking the best in others. Okay showing their vulnerabilities and emotions. Fun... really fun. Curious about everything. Considerate. Classy. Smooth. Funny. Phenomenal at telling stories. Gentle with the feelings of others, but not afraid of confrontation. A sharp dresser with their own style. Engaged with some meaningful causes. Up-to-date on the news of the day. Understanding that all of us have a unique past. Always looking for the good in others. Not shy about sharing their viewpoint, but excited to hear the viewpoint of others. Healthy. Focused. Socially conscious. Inclusive.

While we have your brain working, take a moment to imagine yourself as a small child. A trusted adult is taking you to a busy playground at a local park. As you walk toward the park, your gaze is transfixed on the colorful jungle gym in the distance. You shift your focus toward the giant slides, the enormous swings, and even a see-saw (your favorite). You can only barely hear the distant sound of high-pitched, playful children, already engaged in the pastimes you're now dreaming about!

You stroll into the park—the pea gravel crunches under your feet—and your trusted adult guide suddenly says, "I'll sit over here. You go make some new friends and have fun."

You pause. Your eyes shift up to take in the whole playground and you see dozens of other children your age playing, jumping, laughing, giggling, and enjoying the carefree world of a child together. None of them are familiar. None are your friends or regular playmates.

As you imagine yourself in that moment, how are you feeling? Excited? Joyful? Timid? Shy? Overwhelmed? Scared?

As a child, were you naturally able to engage with strangers, build trust with them, and connect over mutual interests, like tire swings? Or were you constantly cowering behind the safety of your parents' legs? Did you walk up to new kids and say, "Hi, can we be friends?" or did you mope quietly around the edges of the fun, hoping one of those children would invite you in?

Those patterns of social behavior stay with us. Some we're born with; others we learn. But wherever they come from, the way we interact with the world is deeply ingrained into our emotions, our habits, and our self-perception.

Allow this book to help you recapture the innocence of childhood and recreate the social habits you *wish* you had established or may have somehow lost touch with since then. This book is about the power of that child who invites you into her playgroup—she made your day, helped you belong, and recruited you to her world. What wonderful power!

What was your childhood social persona?

Would you like to re-capture it or forget it? Release whatever social baggage you've brought with you from childhood. It's time to start fresh. It's time to reinvent the way you connect with the world. It's time to be the best version of you. We dare you.

Stories of Social Excellence
Building Bridges in Boystown

Andrew Marin is a devout evangelical Christian. When, over a period of a few months three of his best friends broke the news to him they were gay, Andrew's religious beliefs and personal relationships were suddenly at seemingly irreconcilable odds. Andrew admits, he "grew up as the biggest Bible-banging homophobic you'll ever meet."

But Marin had another deeply-held belief—that meaningful, engaged, thoughtful conversation with people from all backgrounds and belief systems could do more to build bridges than fear, avoidance or anger ever could. So he moved into Boystown—Chicago's gay neighborhood—and started connecting with the people who lived there.

"When I moved to Boystown, I moved there to learn. I didn't know what I was supposed to learn, but I figured that proximity would help," said Marin when interviewed. He moved in with two of his best friends (both lesbians) and, as he put it, "Back then—and now—I was just a dude who was trying to learn to live and love in real time."

Once he settled into his new place, he asked his friends what people in this neighborhood did for fun and just like that, he found himself smack in the middle of a loud, crowded gay bar.

Marin recounts, "This guy came up to me and said, 'You're not gay, are you?' I said 'no' and the guy immediately yells to his group of friends, 'I told you! I win the bet. Pay up!' He then came back over to me and said, 'If you're not gay, what are you doing here?'"

Here's where Marin's demonstration of Social Excellence really takes off. He answered, "I have no idea what I'm doing here. To be honest, I'm kind of homophobic and I'm here with two of my best friends who just came out." While his friends shook their heads in embarrassment,

Marin's response triggered a level of fascination in the group of strangers he had just encountered. His level of vulnerability, transparency, and honesty apparently struck a chord, and quickly he had a group of curious people around him, asking questions about what it was like to be homophobic. They talked until the bar closed and left with the promise to get together again and continue the conversation.

Within six weeks, that small group conversation had grown. "It was me and thirty-six gay and lesbian people coming together regularly and sharing with each other." The gatherings Andrew led were not about spreading a gospel, preaching a doctrine, or changing people; they were about diverse viewpoints discussing sexuality, religion, politics, and real life.

Andrew continued to build his social network in the neighborhood with the intention of engaging in real conversation. He started hosting what he calls "Living in the Tension" gatherings at a nearby gay bar. At these gatherings, he invited every conceivable viewpoint on Christianity's relationship with homosexuality to dive into the discussion, learn from one another, and build bridges.

Within two years, those late night bar conversations had grown to 150 people every week, coming together to engage, share, and learn from one another.

When asked how he kept his work in the community going in the early years, Marin said, "Five to seven nights a week I'd go out in the neighborhood with my friends and just talk to people. We'd go to anything—bars, clubs, organizations, gatherings, whatever. Person by person by person, I wanted to hear people's story. Most people didn't even know my name, they just called me Straighty McStraighterson, but that was fine with me."

Marin's work has sprouted a nonprofit organization called The Marin Foundation. Their website, www.TheMarinFoundation.org explains, "We are a Movement shaped by bold individuals of reconciliation;

whose orientation is one of love, who live in the tension and refuse to allow hate, disagreements or past experiences cause division in any community."

"What our work is really about," said Marin, "is being transparent and real—and doing those two things in the context of relationships."

Despite your personal belief system or opinion on Andrew's work, his willingness to build bold relationships, strike up powerful conversations, be vulnerable, and engage with his community are all hallmarks of a Socially Excellent lifestyle.

1.3 SOCIAL AWKWARDNESS

Popular teenage culture created a creature called the "Awkward Turtle." According to UrbanDictionary.com—a hilarious site to reference in a book like this—the Awkward Turtle is, "A motion performed by stacking one's hands on top of one another, extending the thumbs and rotating the thumbs slowly. Performed after a friend has said or done something awkward, either to ease the tension or further humiliate the friend."

A quick Google search provided a clarifying illustration seen here.

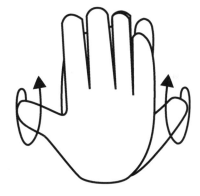

awkward turtle

We're not sure the origins of the Awkward Turtle—we assume some kid saw a helpless turtle flailing his tiny legs while stuck on his back, and then cruelly compared him to some un-cool schoolmate—but we've certainly met some people who could be classified as awkward turtles themselves, considering their unique abilities to be socially awkward in all the wrong ways, at all the wrong times. Before you think we're cruel, keep reading.

Let's describe our awkward turtle friends a bit more. They come in various shapes and sizes and their awkwardness manifests itself in many of different ways. There are the super-shy guys, the ultra-timid gals, the sleazy salesmen, the annoyingly-loud lady, the narcissistic a-hole, the manipulator, Miss Cranky Pants, the persistently pouty pessimist, Mr. Creepy Mc-

Creeperson, the lazy lady, Mr. Tough Guy, the close talker, the clueless clown, the nerd, the geek, the dork... you get the picture.

We list these species of awkward turtles to give you a moment to find yourself in that list. You see, we all have a little awkwardness within us—some of us have a lot more than others. We all swing and miss sometimes in social settings. We all have some work to do when it comes to achieving excellence socially. And yet we hardly ever intentionally work to refine our social self.

Becoming Socially Excellent is a journey that includes a progression from your current self to your Socially Excellent self. You might think of the starting point as the awkward turtle end of a continuum with Social Excellence at the other end of that same continuum.

Below, you will find exactly that continuum, with endpoints identified as "awkward turtle" and "Social Excellence." Make a hash mark on the continuum representing your current social self, and date it with today's date. Come back after you've followed all the instructions in this book and indicate how far you have progressed as a result.

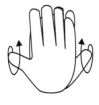

If you've placed a line somewhere in the middle, you might feel pretty good about yourself. You can make it through conversations without too much awkwardness and you feel pretty okay about your social skills. The middle feels like a nice, safe place to put your hash mark.

The reality, however, is that the middle of the continuum is where social averageness is. This book is about excellence. In our opinion, the middle is undesirable, but we'll talk more about this later. Our goal is to get you out of the middle, which is where most people live comfortably unfulfilled. You can't be average and change the world at the same time. Welcome to your journey out of average and toward Social Excellence.

This is Not About Popularity

Important note: **Social Excellence is not about being popular or cool.**

It has somehow become commonly accepted that people who are good socially are the traditionally "cool" people, or are naturally popular. We strongly argue against that point. Socially Excellent people—as we hope you will come to agree—are often not obviously cool, and certainly aren't shooting for popular as a goal. They don't try to impress other people— other people are naturally impressed with how confident they are and the positive energy they bring with them to every social interaction.

If you don't think you're cool, that's okay. It has nothing to do with being Socially Excellent. In fact, most cool people we know think they can lean on their coolness in social situations. They stay in their cool comfort zone and talk to their also-popular friends. They gossip about the perceived un-cool crowd and work for the adoration of others instead of deep connections with others. They often miss out on experiencing the magic of Social Excellence. We often find that people who strive to maintain their popularity are jerks. They don't care about others—only about themselves—and that's not what Social Excellence is about. That might be a little too blunt for some, but please understand our point: being Socially Excellent doesn't make you better than others; it makes you better than who you were.

If you want to be popular—in the traditional high school cafeteria sense of the word—you have missed the point. If, however, you want to win the respect of the people around you; if you think it is cool to engage in deep meaningful conversations with anyone, (regardless of social status, race, age, creed, sexuality or any "other" different than you) because they can provide you a deeper understanding of the world, well... we'd like to sit at your table for lunch today. Let's redefine cool together, shall we?

1.4 WE ARE SOCIAL ANIMALS

We are social animals. Humans, like many animals, depend upon each other to survive and thrive. Humans, unlike other animals, have figured out how to take being social to a whole new level. Our societies are complex and our interactions are multi-layered, yet we somehow make all of that work.

The key, many would argue, is our species' keen ability to relate on many different levels. From strangers to acquaintances to friends to members to neighbors to co-workers to lovers to colleagues to classmates to respected foes to teammates to family members to siblings to countrymen to pals to sweethearts to partners to clients to prospects to seatmates to congregants to constituents to patients to Facebook friends... our social world is complex and deeply interconnected. We live our lives among other people. We are highly social beings.

But are we excellent at being social? Shouldn't we be striving for excellence socially?

If we know that humans are social beings, and we live our lives among other people, then could Social Excellence be the thing that separates people who feel fulfillment from those who feel despair?

Social Excellence is making the most of our social life. It's engaging society so we might matter. Social Excellence is enthusiastically connecting with others in a way that positively impacts the world in which we live.

Humans are hardly the rugged individualists we sometimes make ourselves out to be. We depend upon others to survive and succeed almost entirely from birth. We live in family units, communities, cultures, and eras that are all built from a social fabric formed by the collective experience, practices, and beliefs of the people with which our life is directly lived. Beyond the natural—almost unintentional—organizing effect of geographical, temporal, and cultural social structures, humans have an amazing capacity to progressively build their world around them through intentional organization. We gather together around things that are personally important to us and that improve our lives. No other animal does this.

Oddly, we seem to take our innate capacity for intentional social organization for granted. For most people, their "social self" seems to live below the surface of their awareness. How many people have actually built a strategic, personal plan for their social life? Why don't most people try to learn about and practice being social in the same way they learn about and practice their other, non-social job roles? Why don't we practice being social the same way an all-star major league baseball player practices his swing? Why don't we practice being social in the same way a surgeon practices her technique? Why don't we practice being social in the same way a firefighter practices fighting fires?

When did the average person last work to improve his ability to converse, listen, understand others, experience emotional connection, etc.? How often do some people depend upon alcohol to lubricate their social capabilities, presumably because of a lack of practice and presence of fear? Is society becoming more politically disparate—and potentially dangerous—because of a decrease in social acumen?

The happiest people are those who are social. Recently, a number of authors have shown how being more social is a proven and effective way to be happier and more fulfilled in life. David Brooks, author of *The Social Animal*[1]—a coincidental title in relation to this chapter—concludes that the relationship between social bonds and happiness is closely connected. Brooks states, "The deeper the relationships a person has, the happier he or she will be."

In *The Social Animal*, Brooks goes on to describe one protagonist, Harold, in a way that is related to the concept of Social Excellence. Brooks says of Harold, "He couldn't bring out his best self alone. He could only do it in conjunction with other people." Humans are social beings. We thrive through connections, interactions, and communication with others once we understand the value of doing so.

The most effective leaders, particularly in modern society, are those who have excellent social awareness and skill. Think of Gandhi, Dr. Martin Luther King, Jr., Benazir Bhutto, His Holiness the 14th Dalai Lama, Princess Diana, John F. Kennedy, or Ronald Reagan. These individuals are the examples many leaders follow. These individuals were communicators, titans of relationships and emotional connections, and inspiring pillars of generosity and vulnerability. Our argument is that their greatest strengths were in being *social*. After all, *you can't lead nobody.*

All leadership is social. This statement is an overlooked reality in today's leadership education curriculum. Leadership skills, traits, styles, and practices cannot exist in a vacuum. While most leadership scholars acknowledge the fact that leadership is a social practice, they continue to focus education and training on the individual mechanics of leadership. Social Excellence has the potential to replace the concept of leadership, or at least supplement it in an important and meaningful way. Being social is human nature and it requires us to connect with others to listen, learn, connect, collaborate, and lead.

1.5 DISCONNECTED BY CONNECTIONS

As technological connections increase, those necessary personal, face-to-face connections are suffering. These human connections are vital to our organizational, business, and societal successes and to our personal fulfillment. Yet, as a society, many people argue (us included) that we are becoming increasingly more *disconnected*. Social Excellence is the key to reclaiming human connection. It's the key to standing out from the crowd; the key to lifting your eyes from the screen and seeing the faces of potential relationships around you; the key to turning on-line "friends" into real friends; and the key to building a network of meaningful relationships who will help you change the world.

[Note: This book was written in 2011. This section will likely be out of date by the time you're reading it. But still...]

Facebook is awesome. Let's just start there. Facebook, Twitter, YouTube, LinkedIn, and whatever other hot, new, on-line social media of today are... these tools are amazing! Online social networking has redefined the way we interact with each other. Texting, poking, tweeting, posting on your wall, liking, and so many other commonplace concepts of today's communication landscape did not exist until seemingly moments ago... and something new is added every day. Our need, as humans, to connect socially has been aided to a dramatic degree by these amazing inventions.

So much has been written about the impact of these online social networking platforms on our society that it seems like there could be nothing left to say. There are scores of social scientists, researchers, scholars, and authors writing about the benefits and evils of social media. Social media seems to be the invention of this generation. Like assembly lines, automobiles, the printing press, and sliced bread before it, social media has irrevocably changed our society, and us.

One study about social media's effect on us caught our attention. It demonstrates how significantly social media has changed the way we interact with each other. This study was conducted at the University of Maryland[2] where a researcher asked 200 students to give up social media for a full twenty-four hours. We're talking no Facebook, Twitter, e-mail, texting...we'll stop there because the thought of giving up e-mail for twenty-four hours has some of you twitching.

Twenty-four hours! Oh, the horror! Could they even survive?

In fact, they did. All the participants survived the ordeal; however some failed to successfully complete the challenge. The following day, the researchers asked the participants to blog about their experience. (Yes, everyone seems to recognize the irony in that assignment). Following the twenty-four-hour blackout, the students collectively wrote more than 110,000 words—the equivalent of a 400-page novel—describing their experience. The underlying themes throughout their blogs resembled individuals who might have spent a day locked in a cave, in the dark, by themselves. They felt alone, isolated, and severed from the rest of society.

"Texting and IM-ing my friends gives me a constant feeling of comfort," wrote one student. "When I did not have those two luxuries, I felt quite alone and secluded from my life. Although I go to a school with thousands of students, the fact that I was not able to communicate with anyone via technology was almost unbearable."

The students spoke in terms of addiction to media. "Although I started the day feeling good, I noticed my mood started to change around noon. I started to feel isolated and lonely. I received several phone calls that I could not answer," wrote one student. "By 2:00 pm. I began to feel the urgent need to check my e-mail, and even thought of a million ideas of why I had to. I felt like a person on a deserted island.... I noticed physically, that I began to fidget, as if I was addicted to my iPod and other media devices, and maybe I am."

These students overwhelmingly felt disconnected from their lives, peers, and family without the presence of social media, yet they weren't asked to give up the ability to pick up the phone and call their mother, read a newspaper in the library, or go next door and talk to their neighbor. But the results were as if the researchers had, in fact, done just that.

The Maryland study is one example of the numerous studies, articles, and even books written about social media's effect on America's social fabric.

In April 2010, the Pew Research Center's Internet & American Life Project[3] reported that "text messaging has become the primary way teens reach their friends, surpassing face-to-face contact, e-mail, instant messaging and voice calling as the go-to daily communication tool for this age group," and noting that "half of teens send fifty or more text messages a day, or 1,500 texts a month, and one in three send more than 100 texts a day, or more than 3,000 texts a month."

Here's another fact about anti-social behavior. The Pew Research Center published another study[4] in 2011 that reported twenty percent of smart phone users had admitted to using their device to avoid interacting with people around them in the last thirty days.

Relationships are being undoubtedly impacted by modern society. The American Sociological Review5 published a report that discovered a thirty-three percent decrease in the number of close confidants people reported having from just twenty years prior—from three down to two. In the same study, twenty-five percent of Americans reported having no one close in their life with whom they could discuss important matters.

Many researchers today are actively seeking evidence to support the assumption that "Gen Yers," or Millenials, especially today's college students, have been so digitized, media-filed, and cell-phoned, they're incapable of communicating with others without the aid of a keyboard, mouse, or palm-sized touch screen because they have spent most of their lives communicating primarily through those devices. Previous generations didn't have the technology that young people today have, and researchers are noticing the impact of this shift. Some researchers are arguing that this new generation of Americans doesn't actually value human-to-human connections. We disagree.

Go talk to today's college students. In fact, go socially engage with young people in general. Here's what you'll find: they want to talk. They want to listen. They even want to emotionally connect. They want to connect with others, probably more than previous generations. They're thirsty for human contact and connection. Most importantly, they want to matter— matter to others, to their world, to the world as a whole.

Here's proof:

Matt was on a college campus recently, out on the "quad," promoting a speaking gig that he was delivering that evening about the concept of "Social Excellence" as a key ingredient for a successful college career. Several students were helping to promote the event by passing out fliers and warmly greeting people and inviting them to the auditorium that evening.

One of the students helping with the promotion suddenly came up with an idea she wanted to try. This young woman, Brigitte, started a "Free Hugs" campaign—she offered free hugs to the busy passersby who were all quickly scurrying to class. An amazing thing happened.

She went ten for her first ten.

Brigitte sincerely offered free hugs to everyone who walked past, and while many of the other students helping warned her she'd get weird looks, laughed at, or even reported for sexual harassment, ten out of the first ten people to whom she offered hugs gratefully accepted her offer.

They weren't doing it as a joke. It wasn't some overly-sexual college student situation. It was real. Those students wanted human connection, but since they'd left home and arrived at college, they hadn't received it... until Brigitte came along.

Young people, old people, and everyone in between—they all want to connect with others. Human connection is an innate need. From the time we're babies, we need human-to-human contact and interaction. Not electronic messages shared in an asynchronous timeframe. Not tweets or texts or people tagging our pictures on Facebook. We need touch, hugs, talk, intimacy, care, love, connection.

It is up to us to determine whether we will let our electronic relationships bring us closer to the real world around us or separate us from it. Some people use social media as a way to put greater distance between themselves and others. They can have "friends" without ever having to leave their home—or bathing, for that matter. It allows them to place barriers between themselves and others—to never have to be truly vulnerable or to avoid connection altogether.

Social Excellence is about having a full social life that includes both online and off-line relationships. Relationships that are the most beneficial are those punctuated not by emoticons, but by real-life, human-to-human, skin-to-skin handshakes—and maybe hugs every once in a while. While the sheer quantity of "friends" you can accumulate using online tools will probably continue to increase, what will last will be the authentic, care-filled relationships you establish—no matter the medium—through which you connect.

To be successful in life, business, and relationships, many people would argue you need one thing: salespeople, doctors, community servants, politicians, accountants, pre-law majors, veterans, veterinarians, vegetarians, volcanologists... you get the idea. All successful people need just one thing to ultimately be successful: the ability to deeply connect, build relationships, and genuinely care about and engage with other human beings in meaningful pursuits—the ability to be more social. Social Excellence.

The old adage of, "It's not what you know, it's who you know," isn't really about a person's ability to hobnob with the elite crowd of the world. Instead, that saying inspires the most driven individuals to build meaningful relationships with as many people as possible. Because despite a person's knowledge, skills, or abilities, a lack of people to work with, live with, love, serve, influence, learn from, or sell to, is an insurmountable obstacle for success.

Somewhat Ironic Note: We know this section hints at the social disillusion caused by social media, but we love social media. Be our "friend," won't you? Find our social media (Facebook/Twitter) contact information on page 241, and connect with us today.

WE DARE YOU

Use social media to enhance your "real" social life. Anytime you connect with someone new on Facebook, Twitter, Google+, or whatever the hot medium of the month is, ask them to chat via phone, share a cup of coffee with you, or grab a bite to eat. See if you can add as many real friends to your life this month as you do on-line friends. WE DARE YOU.

Stories of Social Excellence
Changwe Kumalinga

Changwe Kumalinga is a college student at Creighton University in Nebraska, originally from Zambia. A conversation with Changwe reminded us that American society has a lot to learn from the rest of the world when it comes to being social, building social connections, and understanding how valuable being social is to community and society.

Recently, Changwe saw us present an educational workshop on Social Excellence for young professionals in Omaha, Nebraska. Changwe was attending as a future young professional and immediately sought us out after the program to talk about his experience.

He introduced himself and quickly proceeded to admit that he was confused throughout the first half of the program. Why were we talking about Social Excellence? He explained that he couldn't understand why a room full of hundreds of professionals were so intensely listening to and taking notes about something that seemed so obvious to him. It seemed so natural to him to engage in deep, meaningful, powerful conversations with others—to listen intently to stories being told and to naturally want to connect with the people around him. Then it dawned on him.

The reason these concepts seemed so natural to him, but were somehow brand new to all of these American professionals, was because of the communal, tribal nature of his ancestry. He explained that being "social" was how he lived in Zambia. The community thrived not through connections of 140 characters or less, but through real, human-to-human interaction—a true village.

Changwe went on to explain another realization he'd had halfway through the program—he'd only been in the U.S. studying for a short time, but he felt like he was starting to adopt an American social persona. He was starting to isolate himself, wear his iPod around campus, only talk to his inner-circle of friends, communicate more online than through real-life interactions—he was becoming, in a word, antisocial.

In Changwe's words, "In my conversation with the presenters from Phired Up Productions, I found myself unknowingly drifting away from my communal principles. Somehow, I forgot the power of a handshake and neglected the significance of an intentional conversation. Even with the networking emphasis at the Omaha Young Professionals Conference, I wasn't focused on the people I was networking with beyond trading job titles and the usual surface small talk. I wasn't focused until I participated in the Phired Up workshop and realized most of us at the conference had no real intentions to remember people's names and know any of their interests beyond careers.

"I mentioned to the Phired Up team that I was extremely grateful for such a timely reminder to exude Social Excellence and be the best version of me with a communal spirit. I cannot imagine any place in the world where such a lesson or reminder would not be valuable."

Changwe shared all of this not in a disparaging way toward American culture, but with a genuine realization of the cultural differences he was experiencing. He proclaimed that Social Excellence was a vital lesson to remind him of what made him who he is—the true connections to real people in his life.

Changwe has done a fantastic job of staying connected to us since that program and we expect that relationship to deepen. We know he is bringing a philosophy and lifestyle of Social Excellence that is deeply rooted in the communal culture of his tribe in Zambia to his everyday life at Creighton.

1.6 THE TWO SOCIALS

What comes to your mind when you read the word "social?"

Some people think of Saturday night activities: parties, concerts, bars, night clubs, mixers, alcohol, dark lighting, loud music, shouting, smiling, dancing, singing, etc. Or perhaps your social settings are more refined and include dinner parties, soirées, cotillions, black-tie affairs, dinners out with friends, hosting a Sunday brunch, potluck dinners, etc. This all sounds fun, right?

While those things certainly encompass one definition of social, there is also a deeper meaning to the word. The broader meaning of "social" is what we'd like to explore.

Social Excellence is unique as a concept because it is born from the collision of two interpretations of one word. The word social seems to have two basic meanings. In fact, it seems to be derived from two different Latin words:

Socius: Meaning companion, comrade, friend, or person-to-person connection.

Socialis: Meaning united, living with others, societal.

There seems to be both a micro and macro-level understanding of "social."

Micro (Socius): Social can mean being friendly, connected, engaging, great at communication, fun, and self-confident in interactions with one or several other people.

Macro (Socialis): Social also calls upon the spirit of a related word, "society." Social justice, social change, social entrepreneurship, and social servant are all concepts that really have nothing to do with being friendly or fun, but have a larger community and world-level view.

Think about any time you add the word "social" to the front of many common words in the English language. It acts as a descriptor, transforming the word to be more people, community, society-oriented:

- Social Good
- Social Skills
- Social Justice
- Social Event
- Social Security
- Social Club
- Social Services

Social Excellence calls upon both interpretations of the word. Social Excellence is truly found when the micro-level and macro-level definitions of "social" come together in a person's life. Social Excellence is about using the micro-level to live a life that is significant on the macro-level.

Yes, Socially Excellent people tend to be confident, bold, fun, engaging, authentic, and well-networked, but the "why" behind those micro-level social abilities is the macro-level goal of becoming a person who has a meaningful and significant impact on the society in which they live.

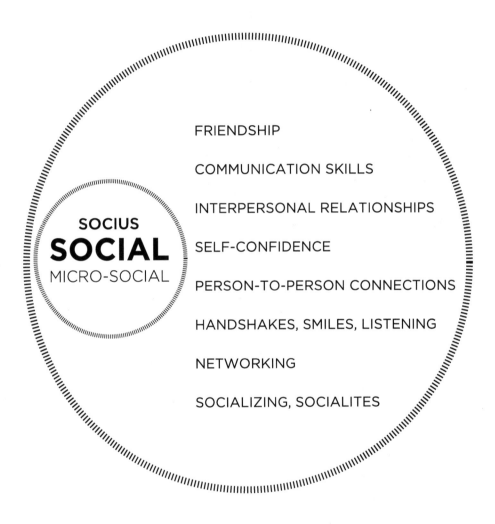

SOCIETY

SOCIAL JUSTICE

HUMANKIND

COMMUNITY ENGAGEMENT

CHARITY, KINDNESS, SERVICE

SOCIAL CHANGE

ORGANIZATION

CHANGE THE WORLD

SOCIALIS

SOCIAL

MACRO-SOCIAL

1.7 EXCELLENCE

Just to be clear, we're talking about Social Excellence. Not social averageness. Not social mediocrity. Not social good-enoughness. Social EXCELLENCE.

Social Excellence represents the highest level of social desire, ability, and impact you can achieve. This book, along with the exercises and dares found within it, are meant to push you well beyond your comfort zone. Achieving occurs when you are stretched, pushed, and challenged to a place where you are uncomfortable. That is where true development, learning, and growth are achieved.

The moments in our lives where we are the most uncomfortable are usually the times when we learn to become better individuals. Average people seek comfort. Great people recognize discomfort and welcome it, knowing that their better self awaits.

Unfortunately, the social comfort zones of many people contain these mediocre behaviors/characteristics:

- Gossip
- Surface level conversations
- Lack of intention with relationships
- Lack of attention to relationships
- Focus on self
- Being overly polite or politically correct
- Boringness
- Fakeness
- Complaining about things, but not acting
- Disrespecting others
- Pomposity
- Conceit
- Rudeness/meanness
- Using others to advance yourself

So, let's be clear. We're talking about excellence. Social Excellence—that will require you to overcome your natural tendencies to behave in a socially average way, to stand up against the socially average behavior of your peers, and make the difficult choice to rise above the mediocre to Social Excellence—not in an "I'm better than you" type of way, but in an "I choose to be the best me" type of way. Social Excellence doesn't make you better than other people. It makes you better than who you were when mediocrity was an acceptable destination.

1.8 Social Excellence is for Individuals and Organizations

"Never doubt that a small group of committed
citizens can change the world.
Indeed, it is the only thing that ever has."
-Margaret Mead

Margaret Mead's quote might be the most overused quote in history when it comes to leadership, management, and personal development education, but it's hard to argue its use in this situation, because, well... it's absolutely accurate, not to mention powerful.

Our company's Reason for Being is connected to the power of organizations (see page 236). We believe that organizations—groups of people gathered together around a shared purpose—can change the world. In fact, as Margaret Mead suggests, perhaps that is the only thing that ever has.

However, it's important we say this to you, dear reader: whether you're an individual or an organizational leader, or both, this book on Social Excellence is for YOU!

Here's why:

We believe that every person is an organization waiting to happen.

"People" and "purpose." These are the two fundamental elements of any membership organization. Get people gathered together around a shared purpose and you have an organization. No people? Just a fluffy idea. No purpose? Just a crowd. Put them together, though, and you've got the ingredients for every meaningful change that has ever occurred and has yet to occur in the world.

We believe in organizations, but we also believe in "the power of one." We think any one person with clear purpose has the power to change the world, but in order to do so, they need to commit to something. Do you know what that something is? They need to gather more people together around their chosen purpose. And that's why Social Excellence is important.

Every person is an organization waiting to happen. In order for any person to make a change in the world, they need to be social! They need to be able to gather, organize, influence, and inspire others to take action in support of their purpose. We'll use the term "organization" throughout the book to refer to the general idea of people organized together around a purpose. That will likely mean something different for every reader. Organization might also mean cause, passion, club, society, movement, campaign, group, posse, crew, and much more.

So look around. Do you see anyone? Who you see around you could be the beginning of a world-changing organization. Look in the mirror. See anyone? You see a single person who could be the beginning of a revolution.

Your Organizations & Communities

We're all a part of many different organizations or communities—groups of people gathered together around a purpose. Below, you will see some examples of different organizations that people are involved in. What organizations do you belong to?

- Teams
- Religious congregations
- Clubs
- Political parties
- Co-ops
- Fraternities/sororities
- Homeowner's associations
- Schools & alumni groups
- Unions
- Associations
- On-line communities
- Groups of friends
- Fans
- Non-profits
- Neighborhoods, towns, cities, states, countries

- Advocates
- Soldiers
- Protestors
- Classmates
- Work Groups
- Committees
- Company Departments
- Alliances
- Girl/Boy Scout Troops
- Members
- Secret Societies
- Support Groups
- Corporations/Partnerships
- Donors

These organizations or groups of people gathered together around a cause are the way we, as individuals, begin to matter to the world.

What would the world be like if those organizations didn't exist? What would an organization be like if you weren't in it? How has your organization impacted the world?

Stories of Social Excellence
The Power of Your Network
Contributed by Jessica Pettitt

Networks and small groups of people have made huge changes in the world. Those benefiting from current systems want to keep this a secret. If corporations, privileged groups, and members of the powerful, dominant groups can silence the impact our personal connections have on the world, they can still wield undue power over the rest of us. This is best explained in the case of Rosa Parks.

Most history students have learned a similar story related to Rosa Parks. The story I learned was about an African American maid who got on a bus during segregation and refused to move to the back of the bus because she was tired. Out of this single act—and a single, lone-acting, courageous woman—came the birth of the NAACP and the Civil Rights Movement.

A few elements of this story are true. Rosa Parks was black. She did get on a bus—every day in fact—during segregation and at one point, was asked to give up her seat and she refused. The rest is false. It doesn't make logical sense, if you think about it, and it's a lot to expect out of a single person's exhaustion.

The truth is that Rosa Parks—a seamstress, not a maid—was married to the founder of Montgomery's NAACP chapter. The Civil Rights Movement, as we know it, had started at least a decade earlier. Parks had attended the Highlander Institute to learn more about grassroots organizations and political protests. She worked closely with youth to develop a sense of citizenship and community responsibility, and continued to do so up to her death.

The NAACP had supported four other bus protests to test media coverage, police retaliation, and public support. Rosa Parks was the fifth protestor. Working together with the NAACP, the timing was ripe for a community-wide protest. Before Parks was released from jail that night, thousands of community members gathered to create a bus boycott that lasted for over a year. A new community member spoke from a church pulpit about the importance of nonviolent civil disobedience, highlighting Parks's demonstration earlier that day. The speaker later became more visibly involved with the Civil Rights Movement. His name was Martin Luther King, Jr.

If it weren't for Rosa Parks's connection to the Highlander Institute community, her husband's leadership of an active network in the NAACP chapter of Montgomery, hundreds of youth that worked directly with her, and the thousands of community members, both Caucasian and African American, connected to the black community churches, the large, city-wide bus boycott would have likely never been started. It is unlikely that one person acting alone could have started this movement. It was, in fact, the act of one brave woman, with the support, encouragement, and reinforcement of thousands. This is the biggest omission in our retelling of the Rosa Parks story.

Parks's network, connections, and relationships allowed her to help dismantle segregation in the south. This took decades and thousands of people connecting their own networks to each other to arrange for carpooling options, a church on wheels program that gave workers rides to and from work, walking escorts, and other programs that supported the black and white church communities, uniting to end segregation in the south.

The connections that made this one act possible started with a handshake and continued with powerful conversations to grow a broadly-connected network. Together, organizing around a unified cause, significant change occurred in the lives southern blacks and throughout the rest of the country. People came together around a cause, a cause that changed their world—our world. It may have seemingly been because of one woman, but that one woman had a large network of relationships that made the cause and her single act successful.

1.9 MATTERING TO YOUR WORLD

In 1943, Abraham Maslow introduced his now ubiquitous "Hierarchy of Needs" to the psychological and sociological worlds. In the landmark paper he wrote that same year titled, *A Theory of Human Motivation*[6], he suggested that people have different types of needs at different times in their lives, beginning with basic physiological needs and progressing through the need for safety and security, social needs, needs related to esteem, and eventually self-actualization. A person progresses through this hierarchy by fulfilling each needs level. The classic pyramid diagram is included in this chapter for reference.

Social Excellence fulfills one's social needs, but we would argue that it has the potential to be a chosen lifestyle that can help an individual fulfill needs on the upper-most levels of Maslow's hierarchy (Esteem and Self-Actualization).

We've mentioned already—and we'll mention again—that an individual can gain influence within their community, can truly matter within their world, and can experience the fulfillment of knowing they are significant to society through the application of Social Excellence. Abraham Maslow seems to have argued this point as well. If one fulfills the Social Needs level of the pyramid, they can progress to higher level needs. Note: "Social Needs," in our opinion, only gets you to social averageness, not excellence.

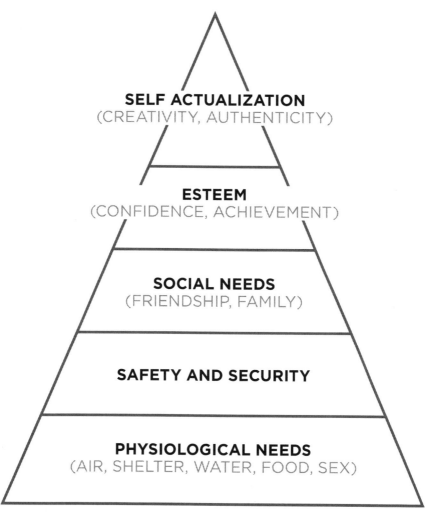

Abraham Maslow's Hierarchy of Needs

If one chooses Social Excellence as a lifestyle, they will have more meaningful human connections, their sphere of influence will be larger, they will be respected by more people because more people know, trust, and care about them, which will no doubt positively impact self-esteem, confidence, and a sense of personal achievement—the "Esteem" level in Maslow's pyramid. Self-actualization is the pinnacle of Maslow's pyramid and deals with maximizing one's potential and being the best one can be—in other words, becoming significant or mattering to the world.

Groups of people gathered around a purpose are what make the world a better place to live because they act upon their purpose.

If you want to leave your mark; if you want to establish a legacy; if you want to be remembered; if you want to look back on your life at 109 years old and know that it was all worth it, gather people together around a purpose that matters to you and go. Change the world based on your vision of how it should be.

All great movements started with one or two people sitting around saying, "The world would be better if..."

Sometimes they started slightly smaller with phrases like:

"This town would be better if..."
"Our people would be better off if..."
"This company would be better if..."
"I wish someone in this school would ..."
"What really pisses me off is ..."
"Why the $#@! doesn't somebody just ..."

All these statements are about changing some part of the world, but ideas alone aren't enough. Many people have dreamy ideas and do nothing with them. True revolutionaries understand two things:

1. You have to actually DO something.
2. You'll have more impact on the world if you don't do it alone. In fact, the more people you have helping, the larger your impact is likely to be.

We started this book with our, "The world would be better if..." statements and, in fact, we've had these conversations over a number of years, long plane rides, lengthy dinners, endless phone calls, and countless dreams. At the end of it all, we come back to the concept that the world would be better if we were all more Socially Excellent; if we could gather people together around the things that matter to us, the world would be a better place.

We want to gather you and others around the cause of Social Excellence so that we can change the world. We want to *do* something. We want to ask more people to help so we can all make a larger impact on our cause.

Stories of Social Excellence
TOMS Shoes

In 2006, a young American named Blake Mycoskie was traveling in Argentina. He went there to play polo and drink wine, but when he interacted with the local children, he found they were impoverished and, among other things, they had no shoes to protect their feet. In a flash of brilliance, Mycoskie realized he could solve this problem, and that was the birth of the TOMS Shoes company.

Perhaps without really understanding the scale of what he was creating, Mycoskie started more than a shoe company, he birthed a movement. TOMS operates on a "One for One" model—for every pair of shoes purchased, another pair goes to a needy child in places like Argentina, Ethiopia, or South Africa. It turns out, people love to buy the shoes, but even more, they love the knowledge that their new shoes represent an impoverished child getting a new pair of shoes—perhaps their very first pair of shoes. These children will be far less likely to get sick, they'll go to school, and they'll live a better lifestyle simply because of these shoes.

The real magic of TOMS, however, is the power of this social movement. Ask someone who owns a pair of TOMS about their shoes and you'll hear a passionate story told, not about footwear fashion, but about helping children. You'll hear a proud shoe wearer talk about causes that are important to them. You'll hear people and purpose coming together in a powerful way and you'll probably want to buy a pair yourself.

More than starting a shoe company—more than starting a charitable giving network—Blake Mycoskie started a conversation—lots of conversations, actually—all over the world. People now talk about their shoes, and other products from TOMS, in a passionate way because their shoes help change the world. TOMS wearers feel part of an organization, a movement for social good.

Like Lance Armstrong's yellow "Livestrong" bracelets, pink breast cancer awareness ribbons, and other items of cause-based apparel, TOMS Shoes, and now TOMS sunglasses, are not about the fabric, plastic, or leather—they're about starting a conversation. They're social.

Blake Mycoskie tells stories about the people he met in Argentina—the hands he shook, the questions he asked of the locals, the people with whom he built relationships who taught him how to make shoes in his garage, and the children whose shoes he gets to hand place on their feet to significantly improve the quality of their life. This is Social Excellence in action.

Learn more at www.Toms.com.

I.IO THE FIVE DEGREES OF SOCIAL EXCELLENCE

There is a theory nearly everyone knows that suggests everyone is connected to anyone by only six degrees of separation. You are, supposedly, connected to the President, the Pope, the Queen of England, movie stars, industry titans, and the homeless woman down the street through six relationships you already have. You might have played the related game, "The Six Degrees of Kevin Bacon," which connects the brilliant actor, Kevin Bacon, to any other Hollywood star through no more than six movies in which they've played together.

Well, we have good news. You're connected to changing the world in fewer moves than you can connect Betty White with Mr. Bacon...

1. **Betty White** was in *Bringing Down the House* with Queen Latifah.
2. Queen Latifah was in *Set it Off* with Jada Pinkett Smith.
3. Jada Pinkett Smith was in *The Matrix Reloaded* with Keanu Reeves.
4. Keanu Reeves was in *Point Break* with Patrick Swayze.
5. Patrick Swayze was in *Ghost* with Demi Moore.
6. Demi Moore was in *A Few Good Men* with **Kevin Bacon**.

Steven Covey[7] says, "Begin with the end in mind." Using that mantra, while we might begin "The Six Degrees of Kevin Bacon" with Betty White, we understand that the end goal is to get to Kevin Bacon.

In similar fashion, The Five Degrees of Social Excellence begins with a handshake and an understanding that our end goal is to change the world. We're not a schmarmy businessman who's working a room and only interested in shaking a bunch of hands to advance his own self-interests. Instead, we're shaking hands with people with the intention of building connections and relationships so that we may find other people to help us change the world.

The Five Degrees of Social Excellence

1. Handshakes lead to conversations.
2. Conversations lead to relationships
3. Relationships lead to collaboration.
4. Collaboration leads to organization.
5. Organizations change the world.

Let's begin by examining each of the components within the Five Degrees of Social Excellence.

FIRST DEGREE: HANDSHAKES

Where did the great change agents, revolutionaries, or even regular citizens with a great idea begin? They started by shaking hands.

The more hands you shake, the more people you'll have a chance to meet, have a conversation with, build a relationship with, collaborate with, build an organization with, and impact the world with.

Most of us aren't major corporations with multinational brands that are recognizable simply by our logo. Most of us are regular Janes and Joes. Most of us are grassroots activists who can't rely on catchy slogans, major marketing campaigns, or getting on The New York Time's Best Seller's list. Most of us make an impact through our relationships—through knowing enough of the right people who can help us put our ideas into action. Finish this sentence: *It's not what you know, it's...*

That's right. It's *who* you know. That was easy. We've already referenced that saying once. That old idiom is a powerful one, though. Many of us grew up hearing that it's not what you know, it's who you know, and that sometimes gets translated into trying to meet famous people. They could help us get backstage at concerts, grease the palms of the right people to get us into fancy colleges, use their connections (wink, wink) to get us the job that we aren't quite qualified for. They could know the backdoor into every opportunity.

Well... maybe that's what that old saying is about. But maybe it's really about the reality that knowing information is fine, having an idea is nice, being smart is helpful, having the ability to do a task is okay, but none of it matters if you lack the ability to apply what you know through people. Relationships are the medium through which our knowledge is transferred to the world. Many very talented, knowledgeable, bright, capable people find failure simply because they lack the ability to connect with—and relate to—people. If people don't connect with you—if they don't like you, trust you, or care about you—you'll quickly find yourself impotent and irrelevant, despite how much you know or how good your idea is.

So start with handshakes. If you become great at handshakes and shake a lot of hands every day, you'll have the chance to make a friend... a chance to matter. Until you've shaken someone's hand, as a grassroots activist— as a person with meaningful ideas to make a difference who just needs people through which to implement those ideas—you don't have a chance. Without shaking hands, you never have a chance to have a conversation. Shaking a person's hand—meeting them—makes it possible to influence, inspire, help, and incorporate them into your legacy of changing the world for the better.

WE DARE YOU

Today is *Extreme Handshaking Day.* You're going for your personal best today. Put yourself in a position where you can really push yourself—shopping mall, conference, Wal-Mart, busy city streets, county fair—and see how many hands you can shake. They don't count unless you remember their names and have a way to follow up. Go for 100+. WE DARE YOU.

SECOND DEGREE: CONVERSATIONS

Handshakes usually lead to conversations, not always—sometimes people are just awkward, mean, or distrustful—but for people who choose Social Excellence as a lifestyle, handshakes usually lead to conversations.

Much has been written on conversations, and there is much more that should be written on the topic. Conversations—verbal and nonverbal—are the energy-filled transmissions that create our society, similar to the electric impulses that connect the synapses in our brain. Messages are sent about culture, expectations, social evolution, behavior, community, and really everything we experience as civilization through conversations.

Susan Scott, author of *Fierce Conversations* and *Fierce Leadership,* has established herself as an expert on the power of conversations. She suggests that the primary tool a person has to influence others—to lead—is conversation. She goes so far as to infer that every organization is what it is because of conversations that have—or haven't—taken place.[7]

Conversations between and amongst humans are what has created our society, our social environment, and our experience as humans. Without a conversation, we never have a chance to build a relationship. Conversations are pretty important, wouldn't you agree? Yet when was the last time you truly practiced, focused on, and refined your own ability to converse? How intentional are you with your conversational habits? How often do you fake your way through conversations just to get through them?

A successful conversation isn't just small talk or chit-chat about the weather, news, or some other low-risk menial topic. Successful conversations are ones in which a heart-to-heart connection is established. Despite the cheesy name of this connection, and the fact that *"Heart To Heart"* was the title of a 2000 book by singing sensation Britney Spears, this connection is a vital piece of Social Excellence. Heart-to-heart connections are those moments when at least two individuals have united on an emotional level. Somewhere deep within the recesses of the brain, unconscious neurons fire that create this deep, powerful, exciting, stimulating, emotional connection. Think of the feeling you have when your favorite song comes on or the shiver you get when the crowd goes wild at your favorite sports venue. Think of the goosebumps you've gotten from a great piece of art. These heart-to-heart emotional connections can be found in conversations as long as the conversation is meaningful and all the participants are fully engaged. Conversations create the energy necessary for relationships to exist. All conversations, however, do not lead to relationships.

WE DARE YOU

Surface level conversations are boring and don't build real human-to-human emotional connections. Many people have been taught since youth to avoid *The Big Three Taboo Topics—religion, politics, and sex. This i*s a dare, so go there! Engage a person you don't know well. Find a way to have a civil, interesting, comfortable conversation about one of the big three taboo topics. Note: To make the most of this experience, go into the conversation with the intention of being the learner, not the teacher. WE DARE YOU.

THIRD DEGREE: RELATIONSHIPS

Most people have lots of conversations every day. Many of those conversations are quick, offhand, seemingly-inconsequential, and forgettable. Some conversations, however, are more powerful than others. Some conversations, either by themselves or when added up with other conversations over time, create something meaningful.

When at least two people engage in a conversation and either person finds themselves caring about the other person as a result of said conversation(s), a relationship has been established. There are many definitions of the word "relationship," depending upon the context. Within this book, however, let's define relationship as, "the phenomenon that exists when at least two people care about each other." Care is the operative word in the definition.

The difference between a stranger, acquaintance, and someone you are in a relationship with is the depth of caring shared between you. This caring could be built from romance, friendliness, shared interest, empathetic concern, generosity, or any emotion that goes beyond the surface level of common interaction—even anger. Care is deeply related to real human emotion. Who do you care about? Really.

Much has also been written about relationships and there is much to be written about the phenomenon of people building real relationships with each other. Keith Ferrazzi's work in *Never Eat Alone* and *Who's Got Your Back* takes a deep dive into the power of relationships. He suggests that individuals can deliberately maximize the relationships in their lives to achieve success in leadership, business, and any life pursuit through focused action plans in order to take full advantage of their relationships. This level of intention and attention to relationships is so often overlooked and undervalued, especially when we consider the vital role relationships truly play in shaping our experience of the world and our position in it.

Relationships are at the heart of Social Excellence. It's through relationships that we begin connecting with others about our true passions in life, building trust, and start having conversations about how the world would be better. It's from those conversations and relationships we choose to take on projects that will make a meaningful difference in our world. Relationships plus a meaningful project equals an opportunity for collaboration.

WE DARE YOU

Connect with three acquaintances. Converse with them until you truly care about them in a meaningful way. Go deep. Keep digging until you feel a real connection. Write about the emotional connection you established and how you want to nurture those relationships below. WE DARE YOU.

FOURTH DEGREE: COLLABORATION

Accumulating deep, emotionally-bonded, human relationships can lead to a fulfilling life. Having the love, support, and friendship of others is often the greatest accomplishment cited on the deathbeds of even the most successful industry titans. "Your friends are what will matter in the end," says the wisdom of the ages.

C. S. Lewis once said, "Friendship is unnecessary, like philosophy, like art... It has no survival value; rather it is one of those things that give value to survival." Friendships—meaningful relationships—are indeed an end in themselves. However, Social Excellence isn't about making friends—or at least *just* making friends.

In fact, C.S. Lewis also once said, "Friendship is born at that moment when one person says to another, 'What? You too? I thought I was the only one.'" That is a magical moment—when two or more people realize they share the same interest and passion. Some of the most powerful, potent, productive relationships established have been between people who had a mutual passion to change the world in some meaningful way—a collaboration.

When finishing sentences like, "the world would be better if..." we often find ourselves identifying projects, tasks, or jobs—things that, if we did them, would make the world a better place. As we've already mentioned, you'll have a much higher likelihood of success if you don't try to tackle those projects on your own. This is where collaboration comes in. Working on something with someone is an exciting step to make a big impact on the world.

When our company was started, it was a collaboration. Two young, big-thinking, low-budget guys started doing some work they cared about. It was fun, but not really very powerful. At first, it was about the two guys getting to work on their project together. Soon enough, the two guys realized that they could make a real difference in their world. They could make an impact, but only if they enlisted others to help. That's when the company was really born. And it wasn't just about hiring more people so they could do more work; it was about clarifying the company's purpose and gathering people together around it—co-workers, clients, fans, audiences, readers, etc. It became an organization.

The initial phase of the company—when Josh and Matt were talking about, dreaming about, and planning to do important work together—was the root of collaboration. A couple of people found a shared passion and started putting effort behind that passion. Collaborating, cooperating, and joining forces to do some important work—this is collaboration—when two people identify a shared interest that is so meaningful in their life they're willing to sacrifice time, energy, and possibly money to impact it. These often look like hobbies, business ideas, causes, interests, shared life challenges, problems to be solved, opportunities to be explored, and improvements to be made—shared action; joint effort; mutual work. This is collaboration.

Note: Josh didn't shake Matt's hand with the intention of starting a company together. They didn't become friends because they already knew how they were going to change the world. Their deep friendship organically inspired the idea for the company. It grew out of their relationship. So to be clear, Social Excellence doesn't suggest you should only reach out to people and build relationships because you want to recruit them to your cause. Social Excellence challenges you to build relationships—continually, everywhere, all the time—because you never know... You never know who you might meet that can help you change the world... or how you can help them do the same.

On a related note, it is important for us to clarify at this point that we believe people join people. We believe most people first become a part of an organization because of a person—a relationship they had. Sure, there are lots of causes and organizations in the world that people care about, but we typically take action within the cause when we have relationships with others who are also engaged in that cause.

Collaboration is about people joining people.

WE DARE YOU

Think about three people you've had meaningful conversations with recently. What shared interests, opportunities, ideas, or challenges could you reconnect with them about? Call all three right now and set up a lunch meeting to discuss how you can work together. WE DARE YOU.

Fifth Degree: Organization

Working on an important project with one friend is a collaboration. Bring in a group of people around that project or cause and suddenly you have PEOPLE + PURPOSE. This, of course, equals an organization.

Organizations change the world.

Organizations are the exponential outgrowth of collaborations forged through relationships. More simplistically, organizations happen when collaborations between two people grow as a result of bringing in more friends to help with the cause. In general, the more people you involve in your organization, the greater impact you can have on the world.

Shake hands. Have conversations. Build relationships. Collaborate. Gather people together. Organize. Change the world.

Through these Five Degrees of Social Excellence, individuals can find a way to matter.

WE DARE YOU

Host a meeting at your home this week to start a movement. If you're already in an organization you care about, gather several trusted members together who could help you make your organization more effective. Not in an organization? That's okay. Start one. Gather at least three friends together at your home to make a positive change in your world together. WE DARE YOU.

1.11   CHANGE THE WORLD

We've used some pretty high and mighty rhetoric in this book. The highest and mightiest—and to some, the cheesiest—might be the suggestion that Social Excellence can help everyday people change the world. That's quite a suggestion. Admittedly, we are a little dreamy. We like to dream big and live in a world of "Limitless Possibility."

This book isn't meant to be a motivational self-help book about how you can do anything you put your mind to, nor is it meant to be an inspirational text about a divine plan for you to do the work of a higher power. Books like those *have* motivated and inspired us to believe that the possibilities for what we can accomplish in this world are, in fact, limitless.

Please don't take the phrases "limitless possibility" or "change the world" to be too lofty to relate to. You don't have to be on the level of Gandhi, Bono, or Oprah to change the world. Changing the world doesn't have to mean rebuilding a village in Africa or saving the lives of millions of children. It doesn't even have to mean doing philanthropic or charitable work, traveling across the globe, or raising large sums of money. Nor does it necessitate a direct impact on millions, thousands, or even hundreds of people. Start by looking at *your* world—the world immediately around you and the people you care about. This is the world that impacts events that matter to you every day. It could be work, school, your neighborhood, your community or an organization. Thinking about the greater world isn't bad—it just isn't necessary to get started.

We all want to matter. You matter in relation to your world. You matter because you make a positive impact (change) on that world because of the work that you do, or the work that is done by the people you influence. We all want to matter. Change your world. Change the world.

In what ways do you want to change your world? (Big ways and small ways.)

SECTION 2

Living a Lifestyle of
Social Excellence

2.1 A LIFESTYLE

What is your current chosen lifestyle? We use the term "lifestyle" through-out this book and we often say things like, "People who choose a lifestyle of Social Excellence…" There is a lot buried in that short phrase. Let's explore it a little more.

First of all, we suggest that one can, in fact, *choose* their social lifestyle. There are many things in our life we can choose, and there are many things we cannot. It is sometimes hard to determine the choices that are within our control, but we do know for sure that one can choose to be Socially Excellent. We'll explore throughout this second section of the book a number of mindsets, values, behaviors, and momentary choices one can choose that will add up to your personal version of Social Excellence. The totality of Social Excellence, though, is much greater than the sum of its parts. These individual choices, as we'll describe later, can become a part of you—your lifestyle.

Within any cultural, socioeconomic, political, or environmental setting, the desire, ability, and practice of connecting with other human beings in an intentional, generous, authentic, and meaningful way defines one's potential for success and fulfillment. In short, Social Excellence does not discriminate. It's not just for the rich, famous, or lucky. Social Excellence is for everyone. This is the lifestyle of which we speak.

People who choose a lifestyle of Social Excellence have a built-in, seeming-ly-innate expectation and craving to be in-tune with their social surround-ings. They always see, hear, and feel the people around them. They sense the energy being exchanged, the emotions being felt, the lives being lived by everyone around them. They want to be a part of all those lives and have the ability to do so. This becomes instinctual, impulsive, and natural.

This section of the book provides some guidance for how you can choose that lifestyle of Social Excellence because it is, in fact, a choice you make. Many of the choices you make daily exponentially build upon each other to create that Socially Excellent lifestyle.

A mentor and coach recently reminded us that we need not ask someone what they value to know the answer. Simply learn what they *do* daily to know what they value. Actions provide the evidence—both good and bad—of a person's core values. What a person tells you will reflect his aspirations. What a person shows you through action will reflect his present state of being—his lifestyle.

2.2 LIMITLESS POSSIBILITY

"DWELL IN POSSIBILITY."
-EMILY DICKINSON

Deep within the souls of people who choose a lifestyle of Social Excellence lives a belief in limitless possibility.

Limitless possibility is more than just positivity, although persistent positivity is paramount. Limitless possibility is more than just seeing the glass as half-full, although the glass of a person living a life of Social Excellence is almost always on its way to overflowing.

Limitless possibility is not about being a blindly-cheerful Pollyanna. It is not about pretending everything is always perfect. It is not about ignoring real emotions, usually brought about by real-life events. It's about hope. It's about a belief in the inherent good that exists in people. It's about recognition that individuals and small groups have deeply impacted the world despite seemingly insurmountable odds (Mother Theresa, Rosa Parks, Gandhi, the Wright brothers, and many of the "Stories of Social Excellence" found throughout this book). It's about a deep, personal philosophy that anything is possible with enough hard work and with enough of the right people helping you.

People who choose a lifestyle of Social Excellence have an uncanny ability to tap into wild dreams—their own and others— and let the energy of those dreams fuel their day. They see possibility at every turn. They realize that everyone they encounter has envisioned ways to make the world a better place, and if they gather enough of those people together at the right time in the right place, amazing things can happen.

Larry Page, co-founder of Google, was once quoted saying that everyone should have a "healthy disregard for the impossible." The spirit and philosophy of Social Excellence requires a humbleness rooted in the belief that one individual is wholly unqualified to determine what is or is not possible. Nearly everyone in history who has claimed to know the limits of possibility has been proven wrong by people who were called too crazy or too stupid to even comprehend those limits. Limitless possibility is, quite simply, a disregard of what is and is not possible.

The Greek philosopher Epictetus once said, "If you want to improve, be content to be thought foolish and stupid."

That's limitless possibility: believing in the impossible and being content with people calling you foolish or stupid in the process.

This belief in limitless possibility allows us to write about changing the world. It allows us to believe that any individual—especially you—can make an important mark on this world, can leave a legacy of excellence, can create the world you want through handshakes, conversations, relationships, collaboration, organization... Social Excellence.

Maybe we're foolish. Maybe we're stupid. Maybe not.

Choosing to believe in limitless possibility might be dim-witted, outlandish, mad, or otherwise impractical in some people's minds, but here's one thing we've learned since choosing to believe in limitless possibility: it sure makes for more fun conversations. Would you rather talk to a person who was focused on limits or someone who believes in limitless possibility? Would you rather talk about boundaries and obstacles, or solutions, ideas, and dreams? Which is more fun? Which allows you to feel empowered over making the world a better place? Which allows for more meaningful human-to-human, heart-to-heart connections?

2.3 DO TALK TO STRANGERS

Your parents were wrong. Well, maybe they were sharing worthwhile advice when you were five years old, but we're guessing you're not five anymore.

"Don't talk to strangers" is rooted in the psyches of many adults. During childhood, when we were too young to consistently avoid danger, many of us had this mantra drilled into our brains by loving and protective parents. But that phrase is a paralyzing prescription for mediocrity and limited potential in adulthood.

People who choose to live a lifestyle of Social Excellence have re-educated themselves to the point where they have a desire to intentionally connect with others... they *do talk to strangers!*

We recommend talking to strangers because...

- It's fun
- It makes your day more interesting
- You will learn new things every day
- It gives you better stories to tell your friends and family
- Those strangers might someday help you change the world
- You might be able to help those strangers with something important in their life
- Every time you do, there are two fewer stranger in the world

Ultimately, people who choose Social Excellence as their lifestyle look at strangers as friends waiting to happen. You just never know what might result from a conversation standing in line at the coffee shop, asking for directions, or commenting on someone's sweater. There is a world of friends waiting to happen, so go ahead and talk to strangers. All it takes is saying, "Hi."

Michelangelo famously said, "In every block of marble I see a statue as plain as though it stood before me, shaped and perfect in attitude and action. I have only to hew away the rough walls that imprison the lovely apparition to reveal it to the other eyes as mine see it."

Your life is a social masterpiece, waiting to be revealed. In a world of strangers, each interaction is like a hammer to the chisel, revealing a glimpse of the art that is your life's work. A life worth living is a life invested in the service of others.

2.4 THE FOUR PILLARS

The four pillars of Social Excellence are **Curiosity, Generosity, Authenticity,** and **Vulnerability.**

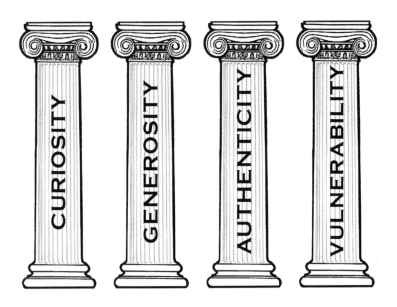

These four pillars represent core values that a person must choose to exemplify if they are to live a lifestyle of Social Excellence. These pillars are not about skills, tactics, techniques, or tricks. The four pillars represent the heart of a Socially Excellent lifestyle. If a person adopts these four pillars into their character; if they pledge to strive to live these four values every day; if they fold these principles into their already amazing "best version of themselves;" then Social Excellence will emerge almost without trying.

Committing to be curious, generous, authentic, and vulnerable will naturally bring out the practices and behaviors that are so often observed in Socially Excellent people.

Curiosity

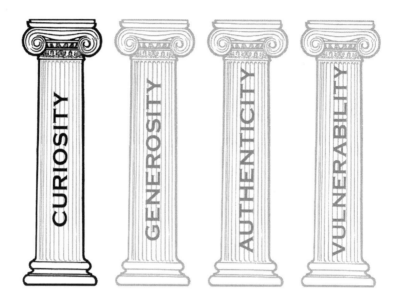

"I HAVE NO SPECIAL GIFT.
I AM ONLY PASSIONATELY CURIOUS."
-ALBERT EINSTEIN

"I'm curious."

Those two words are powerful. They open the door to conversation more easily than perhaps any other pair of words. Curiosity is the first of the four pillars of Social Excellence.

People who live a lifestyle of Social Excellence go through life with an unquenchable curiosity for the world around them, especially the people around them. They believe that every individual has something to teach them every person has lived a rich, interesting, full life and to learn more about another person's life is to unlock that lifetime of wisdom.

The stories we share with each other are the glue that binds together our society they are how we share our cultures, traditions, and values. To show interest in another's life, to provide a listening ear to another person's personal story, to inquire about a person's passions, is to give one of the greatest gifts mankind has to offer—human connection.

Curiosity is a habit. Saying "I'm curious" fifteen times a day and following it up with a genuine question can change your life. You will enter in another person's world and will learn about who they are.

Go to a public place right now and look around. What do you see? Do you see strangers living their own lives? Or do you see brilliant, fascinating, experienced, giving, amazing people who can help you understand your world in a whole new way? What do you want to learn more about? That lady's hat? That man's lapel pin? That child's smile? That vet's fatigues? That woman's frown? That fellow's persistence? That person's book? That kid's jacket? That woman's tattoo? That guy's background? That magician's pet monkey? You never know what you might see when you actually start looking.

Curiosity is a mindset that compels Socially Excellent people. They are haunted by questions as they explore their surroundings. New people and new environments present exciting opportunities full of undiscovered information, possibilities, and opportunity.

How? Why? When? Where? Who? The questions fill their minds. Composed and mature on the outside, they are almost childlike on the inside, eager to explore and discover the life lessons that can be shared by the people around them.

Have you ever met someone who seems to know everything? She isn't a know-it-all, but she seems to know a little about a lot. We would wager that those people are either Socially Excellent or addicted to Wikipedia. Most often, they are genuinely curious about everyone they meet and everything around them. As a result, they learn little tidbits and trinkets of knowledge from others that they meet that they then share with others.

People who live a Socially Excellent life can't help but be curious, probably because it is so rewarding. Say "I'm curious" to someone and you'll almost always be granted that person's time, attention, and assistance. People want to share what they know with others. Curiosity gives individuals permission to teach you something. What a generous thing to do!

GET OUT OF THE MIDDLE

When some people try to be curious about others, they sometimes don't know what to say. They ask questions that are boring, start conversations about topics that are boring, tell stories that are boring, and that makes them boring!

"So, what do you do for a living?"

"How about this weather, eh?"

"So, where are you from?"

"How are you doing?"

"'Sup?"

Honestly, these questions are sometimes helpful to get a conversation off the ground, but they're only average at best. This book isn't about being just okay. This book isn't about social mediocrity. It's about excellence. How often does an excellent conversation, a deep interaction or meaningful relationship, sprout directly from a discussion about the overcast weather?

Our point isn't that you should never ask these questions; it's just that you should move past them as fast as you can. They're conversation fillers. They add noise to the space, but they don't add value. You see, these questions exist in that world of average, boring, and mediocre—we'll call it *the middle*. Get out of the middle!

Other than the creamy center of Oreo cookies, the middle is not anything to celebrate. It isn't remarkable in any way. These conversations are not memorable, life changing, or powerful. People who choose a Socially Excellent lifestyle do their best to get out of the middle as fast as they can and as often as possible. They know that the best human-to-human exchanges exist in one of two zones:

1. The Fun Zone
2. The Deep Zone

These two zones can help focus your curiosity to be more effective. Be curious about people in order to get you out of the middle and into either The Fun Zone or The Deep Zone.

The Fun Zone is not a new amusement park in town; it's a category of conversations—and questions that lead to conversations—that are marked by giggling, belly laughing, stories told with big smiles and flailing arm gestures. They are those moments when two or more people are so lost in the joyful fog of happiness, humor, and fun that the rest of the world seems to disappear in a haze of glee. This is The Fun Zone.

One great way to get to The Fun Zone quickly is to surprise the people you're interacting with by asking Fun Zone questions. You can find a list of over thirty great Fun Zone questions toward the back of this book, and even more at www.PhiredUp.com, but here are a few to give you the flavor of The Fun Zone:

"What's the most embarrassing song in your iPod?"

"Describe the worst date you've ever had."

"If you could punch one celebrity, who would you choose and why?"

The other way to get out of the middle is to dive headfirst into The Deep Zone. The Deep Zone is not a new, special menu item from Pizza Hut. It is a category of conversations—and questions that lead to conversations— that are marked by intense focus, serious tones, stories shared from the heart, disclosure of important personal feelings and information, and such deep levels of listening and caring that the rest of the world seems to disappear because you're focused on each other and the moment. This is The Deep Zone.

The Deep Zone is about *why,* not *what.* For example, most people don't really care what you do for a living or how you spend your free time, but they do care *why* you do it. The Deep Zone gets past the surface conversations and begins to investigate not just the *what* of a person, but the *why.*

Of course, a great way to get to The Deep Zone is to ask Deep Zone questions. Just like the Fun Zone questions, there are a bunch that can be found at the back of this book and on the Phired Up website, but here are a few to demonstrate the spirit of these types of questions:

"Who do you most admire and why?"

"What's the most significant thing you've done this month?"

"What's the most important thing you want people to know about you?" The Fun Zone and The Deep Zone allow you to have curious conversations that are exciting, interesting, and fun. They allow you to take a genuine interest in someone and learn, laugh, and connect without being bored. They help you get out of the forgettable middle.

Be curious, but don't be boring. Ask great questions that allow you to truly learn about people in important ways. Get out of the middle as soon as you can and truly connect on a heart-to-heart level.

*Special thanks to Vince Fabra, a brilliant young man, who works with us and coined the terms "Fun Zone" and "Deep Zone." Vince has a special talent as a stand-up comedian and he lives in either of these two zones at all times. He chooses to be the person who pushes everyone out of the middle and into the zones where life is truly lived.

GENEROSITY

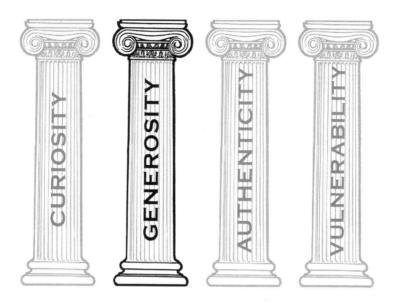

"LET NO ONE EVER COME TO YOU
WITH LEAVING BETTER AND HAPPIER."
- MOTHER THERESA

The second pillar of Social Excellence is generosity. People who live a lifestyle of Social Excellence are truly generous people— generous with their time, their energy, their attention, and their resources. They give of themselves to others.

Generosity normally conjures the idea of pulling out your wallet and giving money to someone in need. That is certainly a Socially Excellent thing to do, but generosity can have a simpler, more everyday meaning when applied to Social Excellence. Generosity is the pillar that reminds us to engage other people by always trying to make their day, week, and life a little bit better because we were in it. Put simply: be kind.

Dolly Parton once said, "I always just thought if you see somebody without a smile, give 'em yours." Socially Excellent people are the givers of smiles to strangers. They are those people who break the ice with humor. They are the people who stop to listen to the person who just needs to be heard. They are the people who give a high-five to a stranger while walking through the airport just to surprise someone with a bit of joy.

Socially Excellent people have been seen starting random dance parties in odd public places (See Dare Card #98). They have a healthy disregard for decorum in favor of creating a blissful memory for others. They are generous. They give the gift of everyday kindness, interest, compassion, and respect.

Making a person's day gives you a chance to interact with that person. Getting them to smile is one of the keys to opening their minds to what you have to say. Want to get a person to care about your cause? Start by genuinely, generously, making their day.

Think back over the course of the last week. Think of the people that made your day.

Imagine our society was still one in which families all gathered together around the dinner table every evening to share stories about their day. People who choose Social Excellence as a lifestyle might consciously or unconsciously set as a daily goal: I will be the person others tell stories about around their dinner tables tonight, because I made their lives a little bit better. I surprised people in some small, but meaningful, ways.

There are thousands of ways you can be socially generous. Send an e-mail filled with genuine gratitude to someone who helped you in a small way recently. Buy the person behind you in line a cup of coffee. Hold that door open a little longer than is really necessary within normal social rules. Thank that soldier or veteran. Compliment that person's sense of style. Help that mom who is wrestling with four kids and a grocery cart. Tell the restaurant manager about your server's exceptional attention to detail. This list could go on and on.

Generosity is more than just these small daily gestures; it is a mindset. Simon Sinek, another one of our favorite authors, recently wrote in his blog (Re: Focus, May 5, 2011 at http://ssitest.typepad.com/blog/), "It's not [just] the act of giving that matters; it's having a mindset of giving that matters. Is it nice to give to others? Of course. But what engenders rapport with other human animals is when they perceive us as having that giving mindset."

If our first instinct is to give, if we give without expecting reciprocation and believe that others deserve our every day gifts, we'll experience the rewards of giving. Sure, the more you give, the more you get. But give to give... and if you get something in return, be grateful. Some of the most generous people in the world give generously because of what they get in return—and the only thing they get in return is the personal fulfillment of knowing they helped someone's life become better because they were in it. Give from the heart because you care and because you want to, not because you might get something in return.

People who choose a Socially Excellent lifestyle find generosity to be a reward in itself. They choose to be generous because it creates experiences in their lives that are enjoyable, rewarding, and happy. They understand that by the simple act of being generous—of making someone's day—they, in turn, have made the world a better place.

Be generous.

Stories of Social Excellence
Free Compliments

College campuses are always a hotbed for creativity and extreme examples of everyday concepts. At Purdue University in Indiana, two students provided a perfect extreme example of generosity in action.

Cameron Brown and Brett Westcott, two underclassmen at Purdue, decided they could make a big difference in someone's day with just a small act of kindness.

"Just overall, making people's day is really satisfying. Not enough people do nice things anymore," said Westcott to a Chicago Tribune reporter who had traveled down to West Lafayette, Indiana, to check out the pair known (eventually nationally) as the "Compliment Guys."

These two collegians made up a simple, hand-written poster that read, "FREE COMPLIMENTS," and then proceeded to compliment as many people who were walking through campus as they could.

The YouTube video that made them famous[8] shows them giving such high praise to absolute strangers as, "Hey I dig that shirt, man." "I like your headphones." "You have a very nice pink backpack," and "You guys are a very cute couple. Have a terrific day."

Believe it or not, this simple act of overt generosity took these two sophomores all the way from sidewalk entertainers to YouTube sensations to guests on The Oprah Winfrey Show and, finally, to a nationally-sponsored tour from Kodak where they traveled the country giving the gift of free compliments everywhere.

Small gestures of generosity can open doors, but it's the mindset of giving that matters most.

THE "SAY HI" PLEDGE

Is there any simpler way to generously engage with the world than to just say "hi" to people as you pass them? If you want to be the best version of yourself, and want to create a tradition of engagement, interaction, connection, and relationships in your community, start simple. Take the Say Hi pledge. Raise your right hand and state the following:

I, [state your full name], pledge upon my honor to say "hi" to people as I walk past them today and every day.

I will do so with an authentic smile and a genuine wish in my heart that they might feel my positive presence in their life, if just for a fleeting moment.

I understand I am not to wink, giggle, or give a creepy stare while taking this action. I further understand that this requires an aversion of my gaze away from my cell phone or other electronic device. I will remove my sunglasses, low-brim hat, and/or earphones that separate me from my surroundings.

Because I maintain this simple commitment, my community will be more connected and, in some small way, I will have enriched the world.

I recognize that this is just a small gesture, but that it will move me toward a full lifestyle of Social Excellence

[Since your hand is up, high-five someone to make it official.]

Generosity and Fear

Does fear stand in your way of being Socially Excellent—fear of rejection, failure, embarrassment, humiliation, ridicule?

What does that fear look like? Imagine it. Name it. Visualize it. Draw it.

Use this space to explore the worst-case scenario that could come to life if you chose to be Socially Excellent and everything went wrong:

How bad was it?

One of the most profound realizations people have while exploring Social Excellence is that fear of rejection cannot exist when someone is being authentically generous. Fear only exists when the focus is on self. It's a defense mechanism—a genetic warning sign of danger. It happens when we are focused one-hundred percent on ourselves.

However, when someone chooses to be one-hundred percent generous in their thoughts, words, and actions, there is no mathematical room for fear.

That realization, once truly achieved, is a place of purity and calm—almost nirvana. You may now find peace, happiness, and opportunity where others find fear by simply choosing generosity

Think about when you encounter fear while being Socially Excellent. You might approach a stranger and attempt to have a conversation with him. At that time, the fear in your head may be saying, "Does he think I'm weird?" "Do I make sense?" "Do I look okay?" "Do I have something in my teeth?" "Does he want to talk to me?" etc. At that moment, you are focused on yourself. That's not generous; it's selfish. You're afraid because of what they might think of you. You're thinking of you, not him.

If you flip your mentality to be one-hundred percent generous, what might be going through your head as you talk to a stranger? You might be thinking, "Can I make her smile?" "How can I help her?" "Is there a way I can make her day better?" "Does she need a high five? A handshake? A hug?" Notice the difference; there's no fear, only generosity. It's not about you, it's about her.

Generosity has the ability to negate the fear that comes with social situations—when we are focused one-hundred percent on others and not on ourselves. Generosity is the gift that gives back. You make someone's day better and happier and in return, you feel fulfilled.

Authenticity

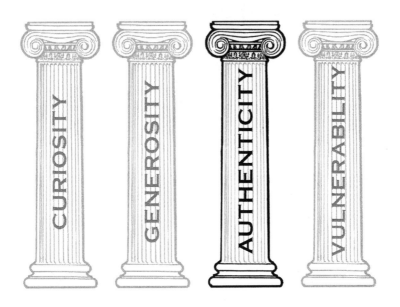

> "BE YOURSELF, EVERYONE ELSE IS ALREADY TAKEN."
> -OSCAR WILDE

The third Pillar of Social Excellence is authenticity.

Authenticity is a recognition of—and connection to—the real you.

Social Excellence is about accessing the best version of you, not some fake, always perfect, sugar-coated version. And the best version requires the real version.

You arrive at this page, this moment in your life, with a lot of "stuff." Stuff that includes experiences, emotions, genetics, family, lessons, assumptions, beliefs, fears, interests, and needs. We all have that stuff. It's real. Authenticity requires that we respect that stuff in ourselves and in others.

Everyone you interact with has that stuff, too. Everyone you interact with every day has lived an entire lifetime full of stuff that has made them who they are. They've experienced the joy and elation life often provides. They've experienced love, passions, and delight. They know humor, gratitude, and moments of serenity. They have held out hope, shined with pride, and viewed something in their world with a profound sense of awe.

They have also experienced the pain and suffering that life often presents. They have experienced loss, obstacles, anger and sorrow. They have pressures in their life. They have fears, both rational and irrational. They have secrets. They have physical, emotional, mental, and spiritual needs—some met and some unmet.

A person who chooses a lifestyle of Social Excellence understands this and actually *wants* to connect with all that stuff. That's the real person. That stuff is what builds real relationships, real trust, and real connection between humans.

While Social Excellence may feel like it changes you into a different person, it will not change you into something that is not authentically you. We're not talking about becoming an altered or fake version of yourself, or the version of you that you think people desire, but the most authentic version of who you truly are. People who are Socially Excellent deeply value and respect the stuff that we carry with us, and understand that Social Excellence allows us to become a better version of ourselves.

It takes guts to be authentic and it takes courage to be your authentic self. It even takes a little bit of resilience. Not everyone is going to like or connect with you—the authentic version—but in order to be truly excellent, it is all you can be.

Authenticity is the "heart" in a heart-to-heart connection. A major goal of Socially Excellent interactions is to connect your authentic self to the authentic self of others. When that happens, trust is established, confidence is built, empathy emerges, and collaborations can take place.

Be authentic.

The Best Version of You

> "Always be a first-rate version of yourself instead of a second-rate version of somebody else."
> -Judy Garland

Being Socially Excellent does not have anything to do with being fake, acting perfect or seeming perpetually happy, acting like a different person or adopting a new personality, or even being inauthentic, disingenuous, deceitful, devious, insincere, or conniving. Schmarmy salespeople are not what we're talking about. We're talking about finding only the best version of you.

Social Excellence challenges you to connect with your true self—the self you truly want to be—and the self that makes you and others around you feel great. We all have that self within us, but we lose connection with him/her because of any number of reasons. Sometimes, instead of being the best version of who we truly are, we become an altered version of ourselves, an insincere version, the version we think we're supposed to be. Maybe one of these reasons have crept into your life at some point and caused a disconnection from the best version of you:

- You're scared.
- You're trying to impress others.
- You're distracted by everyday doldrums.
- You're not confident in who you are.
- You think you're not good enough.
- You think you're too good.
- You didn't know you had a best version of you.
- You forgot the value of others.

At the end of the day, the only thing you can be is the best version of your most authentic self. Anything else would simply be a lie. But do you really know who you are when you are being the best version of the authentic you?

Answer these questions to reconnect with the best version of you. Take time to write down your responses. Feel free to use the extra space at the back of the book.

1. What are three moments in your life—one recent, one from within the last five years, and one from your youth—when you've been the best version of you?

2. How do you look, feel, think, act, talk, listen, stand, and relate differently with people when you're connected to the best version of you?

3. What helps you connect with the best version of you?

4. What keeps you from connecting with the best version of you more consistently?

5. How could you demonstrate being the best version of you right now? We dare you!

INTENT

Have you ever met someone you didn't trust? Have you ever spent time with someone and got the feeling they weren't being one-hundred percent authentic?

Jot down a few reasons why you thought they weren't being authentic:

We don't teach the lifestyle of Social Excellence as a means to get what you want or to manipulate others. Social Excellence helps individuals to discover the best version of themselves to grow a network of meaningful relationships and to deeply impact the world in a positive way. It is not meant to trick, coerce, or manipulate others to leverage an agenda, business, or idea. Social Excellence is truly altruistic—it isn't really about you at all.

Sure, Social Excellence helps you to become a better person, but above all, it's a means to deeply impact humanity in a positive and beneficial way. If your intent is selfish and not selfless, you're missing the point.

Too often, people use their social abilities to manipulate others. There are plenty of psychological tricks that are easily learned and can make others think or do the things you want from them. From brainwashing to leading questions to pushing emotional buttons to passive aggressiveness and more, these tactics are about manipulating people. These are just a few examples of the way people interact with others through selfish intentions. These are not authentic.

Let's intentionally remember the second pillar: generosity. If your intent in social situations is to be generous to others, you are heading down the road to Social Excellence. If you're using your gift of gab, your storyteller's tongue, your perfectly orchestrated body language, or your cunning conversational tricks to get others to do your bidding, you're heading down the road to being a social misfit.

The intent of people who choose Social Excellence is to meaningfully connect with others' authentic selves, to build relationships, and to make the world a better place as a result.

Be warned, though. When you begin to experiment with Social Excellence, practice these pillars, and serve your social community with pure intentions, you might experience some feelings of social disorientation. People will look at you a little differently. In fact, many others will notice you. Be prepared for more smiles, more conversation, and even a little staring from onlookers. You'll stand out. There will be something about you that will be a little different than the you from yesterday, and something quite different from other people in the room.

You may feel like you are luckier than you used to be. You are not only hearing "yes" more often, but you have to ask less frequently. Good fortune is following you.

It may start to feel like your new lifestyle is transforming your world into one full of favor. Be careful though. This feeling of everything going your way might tempt you to take advantage of your newfound social powers.

The tabloids stay filled with celebrities who lose control when the world presents too many temptations. You might recall an ugly duckling from your childhood who became a beautiful swan, but soon lost her sense of self. Again, what will you do and who will you become when trust, treasures, and temptations are regularly presented to you?

Please pause to consider this important yellow flag—this word of caution.

Choose early to stay rooted in your core values and never leverage Social Excellence to manipulate others. Social Excellence is about self-improvement so that we may become selfless in the pursuit to change the world for the better. It is not a selfish pursuit of personal success and a life of favor.

Authenticity is rooted in pure intentions.

Vulnerability

"WE BUILD TOO MANY WALLS AND NOT ENOUGH BRIDGES."
- SIR ISAAC NEWTON

The fourth Pillar of Social Excellence is vulnerability. Vulnerability, for many, is also the scariest of the four. What comes to mind when you hear the word *vulnerability*?

Traditionally, people, especially men, immediately say words like "scary" or "weak," when considering the concept of vulnerability. American culture has fostered an environment where the expectation is to be strong. Our language is riddled with messages of strength, perseverance, and courage and the idea of being *vulnerable* may be perceived as contradictory to that message, often to the point of being scary.

Social Excellence, however, teaches us to engage in meaningful and powerful dialogue with others. In order to do that, individuals must be vulnerable.

Now when we say "be vulnerable," we don't mean to suggest dumping your life problems on strangers. But in order to fully know someone—in order to fully understand them—you have to go beyond typical conversation that floats on the surface like your favorite movies, what you did this weekend, or the weather. You have to dig deeper and that requires trust.

Who are some people you trust?

How do you know you can trust them?

We tend to put walls up around us. It's a defense mechanism to protect us from being hurt. We don't let many people inside our walls. As a result, there are few people in our lives who truly know us—few people who we truly trust. It requires vulnerability.

Creating that trust, allowing the people we know—even the people we've just met—to truly know us necessitates being open. It requires self-disclosure, truth, and unwrapping the layers of outer image we surround ourselves with to open up our inner authentic self. Choosing to be vulnerable can be one of the best ways to share your authentic self with others.

Being vulnerable comes with responsibility. When you are vulnerable, people typically reciprocate by also being vulnerable. In conversation, people may disclose things as seemingly minor as a crush they have or as major as a life's confession. While these moments of vulnerability and the things people disclose may seem insignificant to us, they aren't insignificant to them.

Being trustworthy—being able to be trusted with the information people share with us—goes hand-in-hand with being vulnerable. We can't know what type of stuff people are carrying with them and how vulnerable they are truly being with us, but we must believe that everything they tell us is significant to them and it's important to not minimize its importance. That means maintaining the esoteric nature of these powerful conversations and vulnerable moments.

Socially Excellent people understand the importance of being vulnerable and the responsibility that comes along with it.

You might find that you trust people because they know things about you others don't, you can tell them things you don't tell everyone, and you can be vulnerable with them—and they likely are equally vulnerable with you. You've let those people inside your walls. But why? Why did you decide to let them in and not others? It's likely that one of you—somewhere in a conversation—was vulnerable with the other and there was reciprocation in that vulnerability. This created a trust. You broke down walls and built a deep, meaningful connection.

111

People who are Socially Excellent understand that in order to really connect with people, they must show their vulnerability at an appropriate level and in an appropriate way. True human connections happen when we stop building walls between us and start building bridges to connect us. Those bridges are built through vulnerability. The more people we're brave enough to be vulnerable around, the more trusting relationships we will have that bridge us to our world. The more people who trust us, the more people we can enlist to help us to create the world we want.

Vulnerability is a generous gift you can give to a new or longtime friend whenever you're ready to deepen that relationship. That does not mean it's easy. Oftentimes, it's far from it. It can be scary to reveal your authentic self, especially when you're the first to share or ask the tough questions:

- "It's my first time here. I'm lost and feeling a little anxious."
- "I want to trust you, but I'm scared because I've been hurt before."
- "I'm feeling a level of joy I've never felt before. I need to share this story with someone to make sure I'm not dreaming."
- "Dad, I'm afraid that my children won't know their grandfather because of the weight you have put on since mom passed away."
- "I don't know what you're experiencing, but I can share with you that I've been through something similar before and it does get better."
- "I don't think I have the courage to do that. Will you help me?"

Vulnerability seems to be the key to opening the door to a person's authentic self. Share yourself with others. Tell your personal story; they'll share their stories with you. Connect on a real level by allowing yourself to be vulnerable and expecting it in return.

Be vulnerable.

Stories of Social Excellence
The One and Only Kate Barrington
Contributed by Matt Geik, Phired Up Productions

One of my favorite things about traveling for Phired Up is all of the new people I get to meet. I just never know who I'm going to meet and what kind of conversations will happen.

However, there are days when even the Socially Excellent team at Phired Up is having an off day and talking to someone new isn't sounding all that fun.

I was having one of those moments as I boarded a 6:00 AM flight from Montana to Virginia a while back. I was just exhausted. It had been a long trip, lots of work, and not a lot of sleep. Being up early to travel across the country, all I wanted to do that morning was have no one sitting next to me on the plane and try to catch up on some much-needed sleep. But Kate was sitting next me...

As we waited for the plane to take off, I exchanged pleasantries with my seatmate and small talk ensued. Admittedly, I was trying to be just nice enough to not be rude and quickly pulled out my earphones to try and get some rest.

But then I asked Kate where she was headed and when I heard her answer, I had to learn more about my new friend. See, Kate was in her sixties and single. On this particular flight, she was traveling to visit a friend before heading to New Mexico for the next six months. Kate spends six months a year living in her home state of Montana, but then chooses to spend the other six months a year in a new location... every year! She picks a new location and when she gets there, she finds a new job to keep her occupied and becomes a part of the community while experiencing a new part of the country.

She's worked all kinds of amazing and different jobs, from a river raft-

*ing guide to helping local non-profit organizations, in her new tempo-
rary communities. I was so intrigued and the conversation just flowed
back and forth; me learning about her and her learning about me. The
conversation was invigorating. I forgot how sleepy I had been. In fact,
I found I wasn't at all. I became more motivated and inspired with
each new twist and turn in our conversation.*

*To say Kate was a good conversationalist would be like saying Michael
Jordan was a good basketball player. She was the best! She was Socially
Excellent.*

*We reached a point in our chat toward the last thirty minutes of our
flight where the conversation reached a level of vulnerability. It was
here that my life changed.*

*I asked Kate how she managed to do so much and have such a zest for
life. That zest just poured out of her and what was most amazing was
that all of her energy and stories were about people and the relationships she was able to create. Kate told me she had two things she felt
were most important to her living her life the way she did.*

*The first was that she had five absolutes—five things that were a part
of her life, no matter what happened. As you can imagine, fostering
meaningful relationships with people was included in that list, as was
traveling. I was moved to hear her explain her absolutes and why they
were so important to her. I have since created my own list and have
found it serves as a perfect rudder in life when I have important decisions to make.*

*The second thing she shared with me was that each day before she
goes to bed, she writes down the things that occurred during the day
that she was grateful for. Kate has been doing this for years. She always used the same type of notebook and had boxes of them at her
home. She often flips back through old notebooks and they serve as
a reminder of the life she's been living, the people she's met, and the
experiences she's had.*

When Kate spoke of her gratitude journal, I was hooked. I believe that if we conclude our days with what we are grateful for, we can't help but choose to be more Socially Excellent. In order to have great days, experiences, relationships, and memories, we have to choose to extend our hand and allow those things to happen. If not, we will all have many days with not much to write in our journals before we go to bed.

I learned so much that morning. My life was literally changed that day because Kate shared herself with me, a stranger. She allowed herself to be vulnerable and share some deeply personal things with me. I'm so happy I was vulnerable enough to allow a meaningful conversation with someone who had been a total stranger just a few hours prior. I'm so happy that I didn't put my earphones on.

Before we departed the plane that day—and I have to tell you, a three-and-a-half-hour flight has never passed so quickly—Kate told me that when she went to bed that night, I would be the first thing she wrote down in her gratitude journal. Admittedly, I was a little choked up. It was hard for me to imagine that in such a short period of time, I could have that kind of impact on someone. As you might have guessed, Kate was also the first thing I wrote down that night in my new gratitude journal.

2.5 BEHAVIORS OF THE SOCIALLY EXCELLENT

Beyond the belief in limitless possibility, talking to strangers, and the four pillars of Social Excellence (curiosity, generosity, authenticity, and vulnerability), there are some simple, practical, everyday behaviors that can be consistently witnessed in people who choose a lifestyle of Social Excellence. Many of these behaviors may seem somewhat elementary to our more sophisticated readers. You might read about some of the behaviors and scoff at having learned these things as a child. But remember this old proverb:

"To know and not to do, is not to know."

We intentionally wrote this section of the book to give you a refresher on some of the most important social behaviors you'll need to not only know, but practice if you want to experience the magic of Social Excellence. They include:

- Be interesting
- First impressions
- Second impressions
- Etiquette
- Handshakes
- Smiles
- Fun
- Body language
- Questions
- Listening
- Hosting
- Connecting people together
- Follow-up
- Responsible and respectable
- Boldness
- Healthy people are nicer

Now you'll have an opportunity to assess your current level of ability within each of these behaviors. Add them up at the end to determine your current Social Skill score.

BE INTERESTING

There is certainly some important advice in the old saying, "Be more interested than you are interesting," but to be honest, people who choose a Socially Excellent lifestyle are also pretty interesting.

Social Excellence includes an awareness of—and engagement in—society. This means you should know about the world: the good, the bad, the silly, the important, what's in the news, what's in the tabloids, the news in your neighborhood, and what's happening in parts of the world that are continents away.

The way to be able to engage in myriad conversation topics with ease and have interesting stories to tell when appropriate, is to be curious about the world, its people, and the experiences we live and share.

Read books; watch the news; go to movies; try new technology; travel if you can; experience cultural events; read cheap tabloids as you're checking out at the grocery store; try new things. The point is to do something. Act differently and often.

There are two simple pieces of advice we can provide to prepare you to be a more socially interesting person:

1. Ask lots of questions. Good questions will help you learn about the world around you and be genuinely interested in the responses you receive.
2. Say "yes" to everyday adventures. Break out of your comfort zone and routine to see what else life has to offer.

YOUR SOCIAL SKILLS SCORE: Be Interesting

On a scale of 1 (not at all) to 10 (perfectly), how much does this statement apply to you?

"I'm interesting. I know a little about a lot and have an interesting life."

Circle your answer below

1 2 3 4 5 6 7 8 9 10

WE DARE YOU

Do something wacky today. Find an everyday adventure that you can say "yes" to. It can be anything. Here are the only rules:

You have to do it with at least one other person. You have to walk away from it with a cool new story to tell about something people wouldn't expect from you. WE DARE YOU.

First Impressions

Take a look at yourself. Right now. Seriously, do it. Look in a mirror. What do you see? We're not talking about the surface attractiveness stuff. We're wondering one thing.

What energy are you sending out to the world right now?

We all know you never get a second chance to make a good first impression. Psychologists teach us that we only have between seven and seventeen seconds to make a first impression. Not a lot of real interaction can take place in that short amount of time. A few words can be spoken, hands can be shook, body position and non-verbal cues can be shared, immediate surface-level physical appearance can be observed, and not much else. The initial energy we choose to convey to our world through these short initial interactions can set the tone for the life of a relationship.

First impressions are incredibly difficult to change. That's an important seven seconds when it comes to your social self. Because of this, people who choose a lifestyle of Social Excellence are very intentional about the first impressions they give to the world.

Within the context of Social Excellence, a first impression is really about removing obstacles to meaningful social connection. If a person meets you and immediately encounters a wall, the opportunity for positive, meaningful, lasting social relationships is hindered.

Let's first look at how you choose to present yourself to the world.

We don't choose our outfits, wear cologne, or style our hair for ourselves. The clothes we wear communicate a story about who we are and what we value. These are social choices we make every morning. The way we groom ourselves gives others clues into how we started our day. Choosing to be intentional and purposeful is a way we can set a tone for ourselves and others—we are giving our best selves to the world. The world responds favorably to those that make a little more effort.

Keep looking in the mirror. Now, try smiling. Seriously. Good. Now, pretend there is a person talking to you and you genuinely care about that person's well-being. See your face? That's good. Now, put your shoulders back a little and look yourself confidently in the eye. Look like you're proud of the decisions you've made in your life and send out energy to that mirror that says you're one of the best of the best people around. Send out the energy of a high performer. Look into the mirror and look for the best version of yourself.

This isn't some Stuart Smalley[9] "I'm good enough and I'm smart enough, and gosh darn it..." exercise. We challenge you to critically analyze the energy you send out to the world this week. This energy is created by the choices you make in wardrobe, grooming, smiling, self-image, posture, eye-contact, jewelry, gestures, non-verbal cues, etc. Ask a trusted friend to help you. Push yourself to be *fun to be around*.

Let us remind you again of the value of authenticity. We're not saying you should be perfect. We want you to be the best person you can be, determined by the choices you make every day. Intentionally choose the first impressions you give to the world.

YOUR SOCIAL SKILLS SCORE: First Impressions

On a scale of 1 (not at all) to 10 (perfectly), how much does this statement apply to you?

"I consistently give off an approachable, kind first impression."

Circle your answer below

1   2   3   4   5   6   7   8   9   10

WE DARE YOU

Tomorrow, feel what it is like to make an extremely different first impression than you're accustomed to making. If you're a put-together, professional, well-dressed person, go out in public tomorrow wearing ragged sweatpants, a tank top, and without showering or doing your hair. Are you a bit more lax in your personal style? Then go out the next day in a business suit. Beyond what you're wearing, approach people differently. See what it feels like to be overly formal or effortlessly unsophisticated. Just don't be mean, rude, or foul. This is about testing out first impressions and becoming more aware of the initial impressions you give off. WE DARE YOU

SECOND IMPRESSIONS

Now that we've thoroughly re-convinced you that you never get a second chance to make a first impression, doesn't it make you wonder if the impression or impact we have on others stops at the seventeenth second?"

We don't think it does. In fact, there's an open door to a more powerful, deeper impressions. For the sake of simplicity, let's just call it the "Second Impression." These moments after the first impression require a little more skill, but offer a more emotionally-charged opportunity to leave a lasting memory.

You might have experienced this in the past without having sophisticated phraseology like "Second Impression" to label the experience. You've probably had somebody surprise you or elevate himself beyond what you initially expected from him. Almost like a boomerang, your first impression comes speeding back to slap you in the face with a whole new sense of that person.

Boomerang encounters might sound like this:

"Jane isn't at all what I expected."
"I can't believe how smart John is."
"How disappointing! I expected so much more from her based on what I saw."
"The more I get to know Juan, the more I like him."
"He had so much going for him... until he opened his mouth."
"I'm surprised how much we have in common."

First impressions are important, but why isn't anyone talking about second impressions? It's during these precious minutes that our conversation and behavior either reinforces the box we have been put in or blows it up into a million pieces.

You don't need purple hair or $500 shoes to stand out and establish a memorable, lasting impression if you have the tools of a Socially Excellent person. In just a few minutes during the second impression window of time, we can leave an authentic impression that touches the soul. We can spin someone's world upside down. We can teach, entertain, empathize, engage, and even elevate a person or group.

If first impressions are about the cover of the book, second impressions are about the first few paragraphs. You might be bored to tears or moved to tears. You might be caught off guard, laugh out loud, instantly find yourself transfixed, floored with new information, or helplessly lost in the words of the author.

We do this with great questions, deep empathy, a sincere touch, active listening, Fun Zone/Deep Zone, powerful conversations, and more. Second impressions are where we define our social self—the real person that is more than the stereotype. The key to a strong second impression is to quickly reach a higher level of intimacy, emotional connection, or mutual caring through social interaction. This intimacy can melt away false first impressions that may have been formed, or bolster initial hunches during this time of discovery with a new acquaintance.

Imagine, for example, the three-piece-suit business man who cautiously talks to the punk rock teenager with a Mohawk, only to discover that the spiky-haired teen has a brilliant insight that he generously shares about the man's business. Or imagine the reverse: a rock-and-roll kid approaching what she initially perceives as a lame geezer only to find the buttoned-up Wall Streeter excited to ask well-informed questions about the kid's Ramones concert T-shirt.

Historians suggest that first impressions are a biological survival mechanism that helped us quickly assess threats and react accordingly. But humans have evolved beyond running away after the first few seconds of a bad vibe. People generally love to be surprised by a Socially Excellent person or conversation. It's time for us to engage in deeper awareness and education. We need to be prepared to touch the soul and speak to the heart, win new friends, and shock the world in the seconds and minutes after the introduction. Welcome to the world of second impressions!

YOUR SOCIAL SKILLS SCORE: Second Impressions

On a scale of 1 (not at all) to 10 (perfectly), how
much does this statement apply to you?

"I quickly seek a high level of intimacy with new people."

Circle your answer below

1   2   3   4   5   6   7   8   9   10

ETIQUETTE

Collectively, our society has somehow determined a set of unwritten rules of social decorum. Manners and etiquette are social rules so ingrained in many of us they are almost second-nature. When we observe someone breaking these basic rules of etiquette, we're shocked.

This is certainly not a book on etiquette. In fact, the section coming up on boldness might even suggest breaking some of these rules occasionally. But a book on social interactions would be remiss if it neglected manners and polite social decorum.

People who choose a lifestyle of Social Excellence understand the value of minding their manners at appropriate times. Obeying the basic rules of etiquette that are commonly accepted is a demonstration of respect for others. Creating environments where people can feel comfortable by behaving politely will provide more opportunities for vulnerability and authenticity to arise. However, please don't do so at the expense of your own authenticity.

The problem with common etiquette is that it can sometimes present as overly polite, boring, and fake. When we're focused on obeying proper etiquette, we can't focus on the people with whom we're interacting. So reframe etiquette from a set of rules for how to behave appropriately to a demonstration of generosity as you strive to make the people you encounter socially comfortable.

Etiquette should be about the people you're interacting with, not about you. It shouldn't be about how you pompously have more manners than others. It should be about acting appropriately so others around you feel at ease.

A friend of ours—and etiquette expert—Nonnie Cameron Owens (aka "Mom Nonnie" – www.etiquetteplus.net), says, "Civility is the sensitive awareness of other people's feelings. This respectful awareness softens any situation." Do you have the ability to soften situations so everyone can fully connect with each other?

The best rule we've ever been taught about proper etiquette, whether formal table manners or business interview politesse, is to follow the lead of the other person. Be aware of the other person's manners, behaviors, choices, and formality. Etiquette is about awareness of and respect for the people with whom you're interacting.

Take a moment to consider how etiquette relates to being a gentleman or woman of class in a modern, Socially Excellent way. These terms have important societal meaning and should be explored and defined for you. When we think about social etiquette, terms like gentleman or woman of class can unintentionally be perceived as stuffy or old-school. Hopefully, you'll be able to relate these words to the best version of you, in a modern, authentic way.

What do the words, "Gentleman" or "Woman of Class" mean to you?

Gentleman

Woman of Class

YOUR SOCIAL SKILLS SCORE: Etiquette

On a scale of 1 (not at all) to 10 (perfectly), how
much does this statement apply to you?

"I consistently behave as a gentleman/woman of class."

Circle your answer below

1 2   3   4   5   6   7   8   9   10

Handshakes

As we shared earlier, handshakes are pretty important. They can lead to changing the world. In fact, handshakes might be the magical secret that makes Social Excellence really happen. Think about it. Of all the things you currently understand about Social Excellence, can most of it be done in modern American society without a handshake?

Handshakes start friendships. Shaking someone's hand and introducing yourself opens a door for a relationship. A handshake is a physical connection that bonds two people and creates the possibility for an emotional connection.

But handshakes are more than that. They can seal a deal, make a promise, and demonstrate sincere gratitude. A handshake is the universal trust-maker between humans.

So, how many hands have you shaken today? One of the easiest ways to measure a person's level of Social Excellence is to count their handshakes per day. For years social scientists have taught us that a person can make a behavior a habit with just twenty-one days of practice.

Chart your handshakes per day for the next twenty-one days.

Note: If you have a weak, wet, sloppy, or timid handshake, you've got big problems. But how do you know if you have a bad handshake? Try this. Give a trusted friend your best handshake then ask her to rate it between 1 and 10. Ask for feedback. Apply that feedback immediately. Thank your friend.

21-DAY HANDSHAKE CHART

DAY 1	DAY 2	DAY 3	DAY 4	DAY 5	DAY 6	DAY 7
DAY 8	DAY 9	DAY 10	DAY 11	DAY 12	DAY 13	DAY 14
DAY 15	DAY 16	DAY 17	DAY 18	DAY 19	DAY 20	DAY 21

YOUR SOCIAL SKILLS SCORE: Handshakes

On a scale of 1 (not at all) to 10 (perfectly), how much does this statement apply to you?

"I consistently meet new people every day. I shake their hands, learn something meaningful about them, and add them to my network."

Circle your answer below

1   2   3   4   5   6   7   8   9   10

WE DARE YOU

Give a bad handshake to someone new, pause for a moment, and then ask the person, "Aren't bad handshakes the worst?" Ask your new friend to demonstrate the worst handshake they've ever received. Close the conversation with a great handshake. You just made a new friend and shared a common experience. WE DARE YOU.

SMILES

Smile. Right now. Smile at someone and see what happens.

Cool, eh? They smiled back. What amazing power your lips have.

While handshakes may be the universal mechanism for Socially Excellent interactions, smiles are the lubrication that allows the gears of Social Excellence to turn. People who live a lifestyle of Social Excellence spend their days smiling—at strangers, at loved ones, at passersby, at the mail carrier, at people who are angry at them, at the barista, at their daughters, at the mirror, at that person over there, at me, and at you.

The truly amazing thing is that people who are Socially Excellent get return smiles more often than the average person.

This could be a chicken/egg situation, but according to Dan Buettner, author of the book *Thrive*,[10] "Research shows that the happiest people report having at least seven hours of social interaction a day." He clarifies that only face-to-face or phone interaction counted in making people happy, not texting, Facebooking, tweeting, etc. We may never know if it is the smiling that allows people to be social, or the being social that causes true happiness—and thus incessant smiling—but we do know that smiling at people is a behavior of those living a lifestyle of Social Excellence.

So go ahead. While you're building the habit of handshakes into your life, for the next twenty-one days, track the amount of smiles you receive from people per day. See if you can consistently increase the amount of smiles you get per day and watch how your life becomes that much better over these next few weeks.

You'll know you're hitting this one out of the ballpark when people regularly ask you why you're always so happy.

Important Note: You should smile authentically. Many of us have an authentic smile, a nervous smile, an "I'm pretending" smile, an "I'm not listening smile," etc. We recommend you choose your authentically joyful smile—that seems to be, in our experience, the one that works best.

21-DAY SMILE CHART

DAY 1	DAY 2	DAY 3	DAY 4	DAY 5	DAY 6	DAY 7
DAY 8	DAY 9	DAY 10	DAY 11	DAY 12	DAY 13	DAY 14
DAY 15	DAY 16	DAY 17	DAY 18	DAY 19	DAY 20	DAY 21

YOUR SOCIAL SKILLS SCORE: Smiles

On a scale of 1 (not at all) to 10 (perfectly), how much does this statement apply to you?

"I smile at nearly everyone I see, including several strangers each day, just to brighten their day."

Circle your answer below

1   2   3   4   5   6   7   8   9   10

FUN

Do you have people in your life that have fun, no matter the situation? We do. There are people who bring fun with them wherever they go. They seem to understand that fun, joy, happiness, and cheer are gifts that can be given freely to others, no matter the circumstance. They choose to give that gift generously.

It seems as though every moment, situation, and circumstance has either pain or joy that can be harvested from it. People who choose a lifestyle of Social Excellence allow the joy to greatly outweigh the pain. It seems as though these truly Socially Excellent souls understand that the people around them, if pressed, would much rather talk about the beauty of the spring flowers than the darkness of the spring rain clouds. There is a choice available in every moment to find fun, beauty, humor, bliss, and splendor.

The point here is simple. Socially Excellent people don't take themselves too seriously. They have a keen awareness of the important and sometimes desperate needs in the world, but they realize that acting melancholy about those realities all the time is unlikely to attract other people to help those realities change.

People want to be around fun people. Seems silly to offer as advice, but here goes:

Try to have as much fun as possible in life. More people will want to hang around with you and that will give you more people to gather together to change the world.

YOUR SOCIAL SKILLS SCORE: First Impressions

On a scale of 1 (not at all) to 10 (perfectly), how
much does this statement apply to you?

"I am fun."

Circle your answer below

1   2   3   4   5   6   7   8   9   10

Body Language

"More than words is all you have
to do to make it real
Then you wouldn't have to say that you love me
'Cause I'd already know."
-Extreme
From the 1990 rock ballad, *More Than Words*

You already know that communication is done, messages are sent, and relationships are formed by far more than the words that come out of your mouth. One study out of UCLA[11] indicated that ninety-three percent of communication effectiveness is determined by nonverbal cues. But how aware are you of your nonverbal messages? What does your body language say that undermines your ability to forge meaningful relationships? Why do you sometimes communicate nonverbally in ways incongruent with your verbal messages?

Many other authors, scholars, and teachers have written thousands of pages about how open body language is imperative for meaningful and engaging conversation. Your body language tells a story to others about you. It tells them whether you're listening, engaged, curious, interested, learning, understanding, and paying attention or not.

Think about your communication behavior patterns. Think about recent conversations you've had—both good and bad.

How can you show you're engaged in the conversation without using words?

Here are some things we suggest:

- Lean in
- Smile
- Make eye contact
- Make sure your hands are showing
- Face the person you're talking to
- Nod in understanding or agreement
- Maintain appropriate personal space

But in order to be effective, your body language must be authentic. People are actually able to tell when you aren't authentic or are distracted and disengaged from the conversation.

When it comes to body language, if you have to think about it, stop. Stop thinking about what you're doing and pay attention to the person you're talking to. Body language comes naturally when you're truly engaged in conversation and when you actually care about the person with whom you're conversing.

WE DARE YOU

Ask three people from three different parts of your life (work, school, family, friends, clubs, etc.) to tell you about your body language. Ask them what messages you communicate with your body while in a conversation. Ask them if you have any bad habits when it comes to your non-verbal communication. Ask them to coach you for a couple of weeks on communicating more effectively using more than words. Most importantly, ask for advice on what the real root causes of your body language challenges might be. WE DARE YOU.

YOUR SOCIAL SKILLS SCORE: Body Language

On a scale of 1 (not at all) to 10 (perfectly), how much does this statement apply to you?

"My body language consistently reinforces my verbal messages in conversation. My non-verbals are in synch with my verbals."

Circle your answer below

1   2   3   4   5   6   7   8   9   10

QUESTIONS

Having great conversations that lead to meaningful relationships almost always comes down to asking the right questions.

We've discussed questions already in the section about curiosity (Fun Zone/ Deep Zone), but let's dive a little deeper.

There are three types of questions: yes/no, short answer, and open-ended. Yes/no questions are pretty self-explanatory; they typically illicit a "yes" or "no" response. "Do you like food?" or "Are you having fun?" are good examples of yes/no questions.

Short answer questions often result in responses that range from one word to one sentence. The responses are short because the questions are typically very specific or direct in nature and don't allow for an extended response. For example: "Where are you from?" or "Where do/did you go to college?" or "Where do you work?" These questions are direct, looking for very specific pieces of information and don't really ask for additional information, so the respondent doesn't provide it. Thus, you only receive a short response.

Open-ended questions, on the other hand, are questions that are very vague in nature. They don't require a specific response and don't target a direct subject. For example: "What's your story?" or "How did you decide to go to school there?" As a result, the responses to these types of questions can range anywhere from one sentence to an hour long dissertation because they allow the respondent to provide an open-ended amount of information. Open-ended questions allow the respondents to choose the things they value most and to respond. What's the beauty of that? It's a window into who they truly are and what they value as an individual—a window into their authentic self.

Inherently, there isn't one of these three types of questions that's objectively better than the other. Yes/no questions, for example, have their place in conversation and sometimes lead to questions that provide more information. But the more open-ended questions people ask, the more they learn about the people they talk with. It's a good strategy to ask more open-ended questions so you can learn as much as possible from your conversation partner.

Keep in mind, when a person asks a question out of pure, genuine curiosity—hoping to learn something new from a person whose life experiences they value—the question will often go to an exciting and positive place. But when people ask questions that are designed to get a pre-conceived response—manipulation—the conversation won't end up feeling very Socially Excellent.

Intention matters.

WE DARE YOU

Make three phone calls in the next thirty minutes to anyone you choose. Ask only open-ended questions. Good luck. WE DARE YOU.

YOUR SOCIAL SKILLS SCORE: Questions

On a scale of 1 (not at all) to 10 (perfectly), how much does this statement apply to you?

"I ask great questions."

Circle your answer below

1   2   3   4   5   6   7   8   9   10

Fun Note: As part dare, part to prove a point, Matt once led a seventy-five minute educational session on the power of questions at an association conference without making a single statement. Literally, he only asked questions for seventy-five minutes straight. That's an expert level dare for you, if you want to try it out. ☺

LISTENING

This book doesn't have enough pages to teach you everything you need to know to become a great listener, but Social Excellence requires a person to have a deep connection to *why* listening is important.

Many times, people are silent only to wait for their turn to talk, but they aren't really *hearing* what the other person is saying. Steven Covey, in the book, *The 7 Habits of Highly Effective People*[7] suggests we should not listen with the "intent to respond" but the "intent to understand."

We suggest you listen to learn and listen to understand. We learn by hearing about others' life, experiences, values, and opinions. We understand by hearing why they are who they are, how their experiences have shaped them, and why they feel strongly about their opinions. When we do that, we then have the ability to deeply connect with people—to engage in meaningful conversation.

Social Justice educator, Jessica Pettitt (www.iamsocialjustice.com), shares a beautiful life lesson with her learners when she says:

"Listen to everyone as though they are wise."

Listening requires more than just your ears; it requires interest, concern, and respect for the person with whom you're conversing. People who live a lifestyle of Social Excellence truly believe that everyone has something incredibly important to teach them. They listen to people's words, they observe people's nonverbal cues, they hear the environment within which the conversation is taking place, and pay attention to the circumstances that brought everyone together. They listen with their ears, eyes, intuition, and heart.

By the way, if you are one of those people who tell others you're a "good listener," you probably aren't. There seems to be a link between good listening and humility. Listening—truly listening to the whole of what people are trying to communicate—is probably the most important behavior necessary to establish trust and heart-to-heart connections.

WE DARE YOU

Silence is an understated value with great power. Choose a place or group of people in which you're used to being the one who does the talking—a meeting, a workspace, a family dinner, a networking event, etc. Just listen. Say as few words as possible. Listen intently, be observant, and be fully present. Go for zero words. Go for deep understanding. WE DARE YOU.

YOUR SOCIAL SKILLS SCORE: Listening

On a scale of 1 (not at all) to 10 (perfectly), how much does this statement apply to you?

"I listen at least twice as much as I talk, and I listen intently to the totality of what people are trying to communicate."

Circle your answer below

1   2   3   4   5   6   7   8   9   10

Hosting

What comes to mind when you read the word "host?"

Aside from the biologists out there who are thinking of parasites, many people associate the word "host" with a person who receives and entertains guests. Perhaps you're picturing the nice young man at the door of your local Olive Garden or an elegant gentleman hosting a formal dinner party. Maybe you're picturing Alex Trebek, the host of Jeopardy. Any of those non-parasitic figures are fine to illustrate an important point.

Socially Excellent people consider themselves the unofficial host of every situation in which they find themselves. They are the hosts of conversations, the line at the grocery store, the community event they're attending, the family dinner, the organizational function, the long car ride, or the business meeting.

Before going further, jot down a few thoughts on what it means to you to be a host.

There are several common behaviors associated with serving as a host.

- Inviting people to participate, both before and during an event
- Warmly welcoming people as they arrive
- Taking charge of the situation (not taking control, but assuming responsibility for a positive outcome)
- Setting the appropriate tone, attitude, and atmosphere by example
- Introducing people you know or just met to each other
- Helping people feel comfortable
- Offering food or drink to guests
- Creating a safe, enjoyable, and relaxed environment
- Maintaining the purpose of the gathering. Keeping a fun energy for social functions, or a professional laser focus for a business meeting, for example
- Being gracious, kind, and interested in others
- Thanking people for their attendance and participation

This is certainly not an all-inclusive list, but it does illustrate the basics of being a host. As an individual seeking to live a lifestyle of Social Excellence, choosing to serve as the host when given the opportunity is a great start. As a member of an organization, can you apply this concept on a larger scale? Can your organization serve as the host of a larger community of which it may be a part?

YOUR SOCIAL SKILLS SCORE: Hosting

On a scale of 1 (not at all) to 10 (perfectly), how much does this statement apply to you?

"I consistently choose to serve as the host to others around me, either officially or unofficially."

Circle your answer below

1   2   3   4   5   6   7   8   9   10

CONNECTING PEOPLE TOGETHER

"Harry, you simply MUST meet Sally."

"Judy, have you connected with Tyrone about this?"

"Do you know James? He's the perfect person to help you with that."

"Carlos, let me introduce you to Sue. I think the two of you will have a lot to talk about."

People who choose a lifestyle of Social Excellence consistently, intentionally, purposefully, and generously connect the people they know together with other people they know so that everyone can benefit from the network of relationships.

The simple act of introducing one person to another can be one of the greatest gifts one person can give another. These connections can end up in friendships, collaborations, marriages, mergers, partnerships, or who knows what. Introductions represent limitless possibilities, and anytime there is a hint of benefit for another person, Socially Excellent people choose to make those connections.

This, by the way, is the definition of networking. More on networking can be found in the section later in this book on "The Social Excellence Journey."

YOUR SOCIAL SKILLS SCORE:
Connecting People Together

On a scale of 1 (not at all) to 10 (perfectly), how much does this statement apply to you?

"I make it a priority to connect the people in my network together so they can mutually benefit from the relationship."

Circle your answer below

1   2   3   4   5   6   7   8   9   10

WE DARE YOU

Find someone you know that is in sales, marketing, human resources, owns a business, or belongs to a religious, civic, or community group. Ask them this question and watch them light up: "I meet a lot of great people. You know I think the world of you and the work you're doing. What question can I ask new friends so I'll know if they're someone that I should connect you with to help advance your cause?"

If you go one step further and begin connecting good people together, you'll become the "connector" through which world change—large and small—occurs. WE DARE YOU.

Stories of Social Excellence
Frank, Ryan, and Coach Herm
Contributed by Matt Geik, Phired Up Productions

Not long ago, I was assisting one of Phired Up's national clients with their interview process. The organization was hiring two new professionals whose primary responsibility was to develop new markets for their organization through connecting people around a common purpose.

After an intense, interactive, two-day interview process, it was time to head to the airport to return home. Coincidentally, two of the applicants, Frank and Ryan, were on the same flight as I was. While checking in for my flight alongside Frank and Ryan, I noticed that former NFL player, head coach and now ESPN analyst, Herm Edwards, was in front of us as we were going through security.

During the previous two days of interviews, much of what the candidates, including Frank and Ryan, were asked to do was to demonstrate their ability to be social, to connect with people, and to have meaningful conversations with new friends. Naturally, it was my role to demonstrate these behaviors to the candidates. Throughout the interview process, I had also learned that Frank and Ryan were both big sports fans; Frank loved his Chicago Blackhawks and Ryan loved any of his teams from Philly.

Seeing a public figure like Coach Herm Edwards seemed like a perfect opportunity to continue the demonstration of Social Excellence. So I approached Coach Edwards and an exciting conversation began. While Coach and I talked for the next twenty-five minutes, we covered everything from the 5:00 AM workouts he is notorious for, to his days coaching the New York Jets and the Kansas City Chiefs, to whether he wanted to coach again, to his thoughts on my beloved Detroit Lions. He even touched on his family, the charity golf outing in California he was headed toward, and how he ended up working at ESPN. Meanwhile,

Frank and Ryan kept their distance with their mouths agape in what looked like shock that I could have such an authentic conversation with the always intense Coach.

I was listening to Coach Edwards tell me how he had landed his job at ESPN when a beautiful moment happened. When I asked him how he he'd decided to do TV work for ESPN, his answer was very simple. "I just made a phone call to someone I knew and the next day I had the job." At that moment, I asked Coach if I could introduce him to my two friends.

I told Frank and Ryan what Coach and I had been discussing and then asked him this question: "Coach, is it safe to say that because of the relationships you built during your years as a player and coach in the NFL, those relationships allowed you to make the phone call that day?" His response was a simple, "Without a doubt." I proceeded to tell Coach about Frank and Ryan's job description and the importance of building relationships. Three, two, one, takeoff! Coach went into what felt like motivational speaker mode and was suddenly, passionately, and poignantly sharing with us just how important he believes the power of developing meaningful relationships is for the purpose of both business and personal well-being.

Coach Edward's flight began to board and we said goodbye, thank you, and good luck while shaking hands. Young Frank and Ryan were in awe and I felt like I couldn't have scripted a better learning moment. Frank and Ryan were able to see the power of Social Excellence first hand that day in the Kansas City airport. While I know I was responsible for making that experience happen, the real magic happened because Coach Edwards demonstrated what generosity and authenticity are really about.

Months later, I met up with both Frank and Ryan on the road while they were in the middle of a project (yes, they both got the job). Sure enough, here were two young men, fresh out of college, and in their first job, they were being more successful in their roles than any of their predecessors had ever been. When we met up, I asked them what they were doing to be successful. They both answered, "Just being Socially Excellent, Matt. Hey, you have to meet this guy we're talking to..."

FOLLOW-UP

As you know, handshakes lead to conversations, conversations lead to relationships, relationships lead to collaboration, collaboration leads to organization, and organizations change the world.

However, that world change doesn't happen because you shake someone's hand once. Change doesn't occur because you had one conversation with someone or because you had one relationship or collaboration. You can't change the world unless you are continually developing, growing, and maintaining your already-existing relationships, friendships, and acquaintances, as well as following-up to build relationships with people you've met.

This book was not written to teach individuals how to meet people, use them, and then dispose of the relationship. People who are Socially Excellent grow and nurture a network of meaningful relationships around them. We know meaningful relationships take work and follow-up to develop, and they take even more work to maintain, but being Socially Excellent means making an investment in people and in relationships.

The capital you're investing, in this case, is social capital—people. Any novice financial investor understands that in order to maximize your investment's potential, you must invest in long-term commitments to create a beneficial return in the end. This concept applies to relationships, as well. You have to work at it over the long-term to yield the great return of deep, meaningful friendships, relationships, and collaboration.

YOUR SOCIAL SKILLS SCORE: Follow-Up

On a scale of 1 (not at all) to 10 (perfectly), how much does this statement apply to you?

"I consistently and continually work to maintain my current relationships along with building new friendships."

Circle your answer below

1   2   3   4   5   6   7   8   9   10

RESPONSIBLE AND RESPECTABLE

Who are the people in your life that you respect? Look back to page 23 where you wrote down people who you think model the definition of Social Excellence: Are they the same people?

Choosing to lead a Socially Excellent lifestyle requires a high level of responsibility and respectability. When you are Socially Excellent, you understand what is and isn't socially appropriate. You understand etiquette and you care for others, their possessions, their feelings, and their experience. You are naturally responsible because you authentically care.

Additionally, you are a model for others. You set the tone of every meeting, event, and environment. Your behavior, demeanor, and attitude are what others respect and desire to emulate. Socially Excellent people haven't demanded that people respect them; they've earned the respect of others because they model curiosity, generosity, authenticity, and vulnerability.

YOUR SOCIAL SKILLS SCORE:
Responsible and Respectable

On a scale of 1 (not at all) to 10 (perfectly), how much does this statement apply to you?

"I consistently behave in a responsible and respectable manner—a manner that allows me no regrets for my behavior."

Circle your answer below

1   2   3   4   5   6   7   8   9   10

BOLDNESS

Be bold. Tennis great Billie Jean King once said, "Be bold. If you're going to make an error, make a doozy and don't be afraid to hit the ball." Without boldness, you've achieved nothing but mediocrity and averageness, and you've created no meaningful change. Those who choose Social Excellence understand that boldness is a core tenant

The world doesn't need more mediocrity. Change doesn't require us to maintain the status quo. Great change requires us to boldly step forward into the unknown in pursuit of a better world. People will probably tell you that you can't, that you're silly for believing you can, and that you'll never succeed. Boldness means doing it anyway because failing to try is just as bad as trying and failing.

Boldness is not, however, insubordination, disrespect, or disregard for others, their feelings, their safety, or their livelihood. It is a healthy disregard for the impossible, the status quo, and standard convention. It's laughing in the face of fear. It's the attitude of "not good enough." It's the borderline insane mentality of "just do it."

People who've reached the pinnacle of Social Excellence thrive on bold choices. They understand that in order to create the world they want requires much more than gathering others together around a cause. They must bond those individuals together to take bold action for change and leap out into the darkness for the sake of a better world.

YOUR SOCIAL SKILLS SCORE: Boldness

On a scale of 1 (not at all) to 10 (perfectly), how much does this statement apply to you?

"I am audacious. I am bold."

Circle your answer below

1   2   3   4   5   6   7   8   9   10

HEALTHY PEOPLE ARE NICER

We are not going to launch into a rant about fitness, nutrition, healthy sleeping habits, or physical well-being. But if we're going to talk about a lifestyle of Social Excellence, we should honor the fact that a person's over-all health and well-being will impact their social life, and vice-versa.

We won't write much on this topic, but we will say this:

When you're tired, you're probably grumpier.

When you're hungry, you're probably grumpier.

When you're generally unhealthy, you're probably grumpier.

Grumpy people aren't Socially Excellent. If you want to be Socially Excellent, you have to take care of yourself.

There we said it. We won't lecture you. We won't tell you to go for a jog right now or to put out your cigarette or to put down that triple cheeseburger. We'll just say to do everything you can to not be grumpy, which may require you to make more healthy life decisions.

Side Note: The research is mixed on whether healthiness leads to happiness or happiness makes one healthier, but one article from The University of Chicago Magazine quoted psychologist John Cacioppo's findings that twenty percent of Americans are unhappy at any given time due to social isolation. And there are studies that suggest that isolation and loneliness can affect our physical health. Lab rats put into social isolation were more likely to develop cancerous tumors, for instance.[12] So perhaps you should just go out and exercise and eat healthy with others, just to be safe.

YOUR SOCIAL SKILLS SCORE: Healthy People are Nicer

On a scale of 1 (not at all) to 10 (perfectly), how much does this statement apply to you?

"My physical health is a representation of 'The Best Version of Me.'"

Circle your answer below

1   2   3   4   5   6   7   8   9   10

Total Social Skills Score

Tally up your total Social Skills Score from this section.

Be Interesting	
First Impressions	
Second Impressions	
Etiquette	
Handshakes	
Smiles	
Fun	
Body Language	
Questions	
Listening	
Hosting	
Connecting People Together	
Follow-Up	
Responsible & Respectable	
Boldness	
Healthy People are Nicer	
TOTAL (out of 160)	

Even a person who chooses a Socially Excellent lifestyle probably doesn't score 160/160 for their personal Social Skills Score. Each of these behaviors measured in this section require a continual pursuit of excellence.

Use your score to motivate you to practice each of these behaviors every day. Ask for help. Learn from others who score higher than you. Challenge yourself. Dare yourself to continually increase your own personal score. Curious how your score compares to others? Tweet your Social Skills Score to #SocialExcellence and enjoy connecting with others.

2.6 POWERFUL CONVERSATIONS

Have you ever had a conversation where you deeply connected with someone to the point where you completely lost track of time? Or perhaps you've had a conversation where you found your new best friend, soul mate, or life partner? You might even remember a conversation you had where you left feeling empowered to do something important or to be a better person. Maybe you can think of a conversation that actually changed the direction of your entire life.

Powerful Conversations transform people and relationships. They turn strangers into friends, friends into best friends, and even strangers into life partners. These are the conversations we remember the most from our lives. These are the magical moments of living we tell stories about years later. These are the instances of deep connection that make us who we are.

Wouldn't you like to have more of those? If you had more powerful conversations, couldn't you have deeper relationships, more stories to tell, and be able to influence more people to help you change the world?

Conversations done right are key components of the Social Excellence lifestyle and they deserve more exploration. Let's look at three different levels of conversation: casual, good, and powerful.

There are thousands of people around you on any given day—walking past, standing near, driving by, shopping next to, working out in close proximity to, reading in the vicinity of, etc. You don't talk to at least ninety-five percent of them. Choosing to engage with someone allows you into the first ring of what we call the "Inner Circles of Conversation."

That first circle—the "casual conversation" circle—has a thin barrier keeping people from breaching it. That barrier is simply a willingness on your part to choose to engage with those people. Engage and you'll find yourself starting a conversation with someone and you know where that can lead—changing the world.

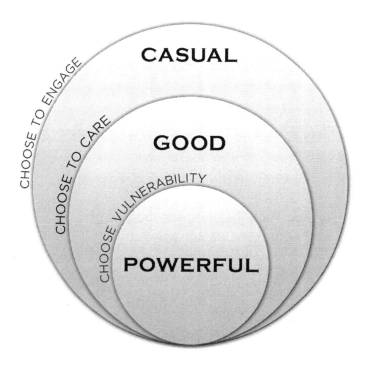

Inner Circles of Conversation

Casual conversations about the weather and other mundane topics rarely result in any level of lasting relationship. This outer circle of connection typically produces passing, unmemorable encounters.

The easiest way to break the next barrier and cross the threshold into "good conversations" is to care. Good conversations create acquaintances and sometimes even friends. They require a relationship level created by caring about the conversation topic and the people in the conversation with you. Most people would admit they don't really care about the content of those outer-level, casual chit-chats, but as soon as some spark of mutual commonality, chemistry, or genuine curiosity is lit, good conversations erupt. Now we are entering the "inner circles of conversation." But still we fall just short of the deepest circle—powerful conversations.

To break the final, thickest barrier and enter this deepest level, this innermost circle of trust with another person, requires one additional ingredient. But we'll get to that in a moment.

First, let's look at the diagram of the "inner circles of conversation" one more time. The more frequently you choose to engage, care, and be vulnerable, the faster you'll move through those barriers keeping you from the deepest circles of connection with others. Getting to the core of another person—engaging in a powerful conversation—allows the deepest level of heart-to-heart connection to occur.

Now, back to powerful conversations. To most people, there seems to be no obvious formula for powerful conversations. They usually just seem to happen out of thin air, and most of the time, you can't remember why or pinpoint how. We happen to know how to create them. We've discovered the key ingredients; one in particular.

The three key ingredients people who choose to live a lifestyle of Social Excellence utilize to create powerful conversations are:

1. **Vulnerability**
2. Intense Presence
3. Emotional Allowance

We've discussed the power of vulnerability, but it is worth mentioning again, lest you forgot or subconsciously buried it away out of fear. **Every powerful conversation you have ever had has included a significant amount of vulnerability.** Read that sentence again and let it sink in. If it is true, and we believe it is, we urge you to consider creating more moments of vulnerability in your life so you may have the opportunity to experience more of those powerful, transformative, life-changing conversations.

The second ingredient in powerful conversations is the ability to be intensely present in a given moment, not distracted by shiny things around you, problems from earlier in the day, or plans for later this week. Focus on the moment, right here, right now. People who are Socially Excellent practice zoning in on a conversation, a person, a moment. They choose to be there. Intense presence is a combination of pure curiosity and genuine generosity—wanting to learn at the same time as you want to help another person.

The third ingredient in powerful conversations is the knack for sinking into the emotional flow of a conversation. This includes the ability to allow the emotional heart-to-heart connection between people to take over and drive the conversation—not a logical exchange of information; not a tit-for-tat dialogue; not an equal trading of thoughts; but a natural flow of communication that seems to wash over the moment and allow for authenticity to truly emerge from within everyone in the conversation.

This emotional allowance means sometimes reserving a question, comment, or story for the sake of not derailing the conversation or interrupting someone. It is intuitively knowing what is most important in the conversation and allowing it to happen naturally.

It is important to note that these powerful conversations typically happen in either the Deep Zone or the Fun Zone, not exclusively in the Deep Zone as many might initially think. These powerful conversations involve a wide variety of topics with a wide range of emotions.

These are highly advanced communication skills that take practice, require a release of fear for many people, and may be hard to achieve, but they serve as an excellent target for a person who wants to live a Socially Excellent lifestyle.

To close this section, we'd like to share a brief story. We opened this section by saying that powerful conversations "turn strangers into friends, friends into best friends, or even strangers into life partners." To prove this is true, the very first time we taught a workshop on powerful conversations, we were working with a group of about 150 young professionals. We encouraged them in random conversation pairings and pushed them to be authentic and deeply vulnerable with their new acquaintance. Six months later, we got a message from one of the attendees. The stranger he had been paired up with that day was now his fiancé. We won't guarantee you'll find the love of your life through powerful conversations, but Matt David and his new bride, Hilary, have proven it has that potential.

Stories of Social Excellence
Confident College Women
Contributed by Jessica Gendron Williams

At Phired Up, we do a lot of work with a certain type of organization: college sororities. I began working with a group of wonderful women in March of last year at a university in California. These women were struggling to recruit many high-quality women to their cause, mainly because, in my opinion, they didn't believe in themselves, individually or collectively. They believed they were failures because everyone treated them that way.

But these women weren't failures: They were highly intelligent, beautiful, fun, caring, open and authentic women - with (sadly) very low self-esteem.

When we worked with them, we focused much of our education on teaching these women social skills so they knew how to make friends. Basic things like how to shake hands and to keep conversation flowing were covered, but they also learned about being curious, authentic, generous, and vulnerable. They learned what it means to be the best version of themselves. They learned how to be open, kind, and bold. The transformation was remarkable.

Through that process, these women found confidence. But it went much further than that. Suddenly, they were excited, outgoing, proud, and engaging. They believed in themselves, their abilities, and in each other. There is now energy, life, laughter, and lots of noise in their chapter house.

Women who were once uncomfortable talking to me are now texting me to let me know they talked to the cute boys they sit next to in class and have set a time to have coffee or dinner with them. They're sending me e-mails with stories of approaching strangers on campus to ask what they're reading, engaging in intelligent conversation, and thus making a friend.

Recently, I made another visit to campus to work with them. I gave them several social challenges. One of the challenges was to "make eye contact with, smile at, and say hello to twenty-five strangers." Text messages poured in that day about how good it felt to make someone's day—to get them to smile back.

During this visit, I also gave them some of Phired Up's Social Excellence Dare Cards and asked them to complete them, and then write a reflection about the experience. I'd like to share one of the responses with you to fully illustrate the transformation:

The dare I chose to complete was to look for a Facebook friend who I don't really know or haven't really talked to and to get to know them. I randomly chose a girl whom I had met the first week of school. We exchanged numbers but never ended up hanging out and I hadn't talked to her since then. So I texted her and asked if she wanted to get lunch this week. We met yesterday for around forty-five minutes, and even though I had been scared I wouldn't remember what she looked like or that it would be awkward, it really wasn't bad! I found that conversation flowed pretty easily, partially because she is really nice and is interested in joining the band which I'm a part of, but also because I used some of what I had learned about making conversation during recruitment and had been working on it as a chapter.

I'm so glad I did this because we found some things we had in common and are now planning to go to some events together. We get along very well and I can definitely see us growing closer as time goes on. I look forward to meeting some of her friends and introducing her to mine. It's very important to me that I have friends in different groups.

At first, I thought this dare would be too challenging and there wasn't anyone who would be willing to go along with it, since I hadn't experienced anything like it before. But it showed me how accommodating people are if you just make a little bit of effort. I am proud of *myself for completing the challenge and I know I'm going to continue to reap the benefits!*

Thank you,

Leah

These women would have never considered this request when we'd first started working with them. They would have been too shy with too little confidence to even consider talking to a stranger. Now they meet and engage with new people every day—trust me I get the text messages). We gave them permission to be their true, authentic selves, we urged them to challenge each other to be the best version of themselves every day, and taught them the skills necessary to be the best they could be. These women are confident. They believe in themselves and they believe in each other. Because of this renewed self-esteem, they are more easily able to find more women on campus to engage in their cause, their sorority.

MOMENTARY CHOICES

"WATCH YOUR THOUGHTS, FOR THEY BECOME WORDS.
WATCH YOUR WORDS, FOR THEY BECOME ACTIONS.
WATCH YOUR ACTIONS, FOR THEY BECOME HABITS.
WATCH YOUR HABITS, FOR THEY BECOME CHARACTER.
WATCH YOUR CHARACTER, FOR IT BECOMES YOUR DESTINY."

-UNKNOWN

Right now, you have a choice to make. Every "right now" is a choice. How will you engage with the social world around you? Will you shake that hand? Will you smile at her? Will you hold the door? Will you offer to help? Will you ask the question that matters? Will you be real? Will you allow yourself to express what you really feel? Will you turn the conversation to important matters? Will you go engage? Will you matter in that person's life today?

These momentary choices are what life is made of. Because those choices add up and eventually become patterns of behavior. Your everyday habits are built upon your momentary choices.

Those patterns of behavior are what you're made of. Your reputation and character are built by those patterns. No single choice defines you, but every choice is a part of that larger pattern. Eventually, those patterns become so routine they become seemingly implanted on your DNA. Eventually, they become your lifestyle.

This section is about choices—momentary choices that become patterns of behavior, and eventually a lifestyle.

What choices have you made today in your social life? How have they impacted your day?

CHOICES I'VE MADE	IMPACT ON MY DAY/LIFE

How You Show Up

Life is a series of choices. One of those choices is how you "show up." What attitude do you choose? What type of person do you choose to be? What type of impact do you choose to make? The reality is that how you show up impacts every person you encounter. You're contagious.

In the book, *Social Intelligence*,[13] Daniel Goleman discusses empirical evidence that supports the fact that your emotions are contagious. Humans actually have the ability to read another human's emotions and not only understand what they are, but also feel them. Faster than our brain can process that someone is smiling, we feel happy. Faster than we know someone is crying, we feel sad.

That means the attitude you choose at every moment has the ability to impact someone else. Choosing to smile as you get on the bus could cause another passenger to feel happy. Unknowingly scowling while staring off into space could actually cause someone to feel angry or sad. How you show up each day—each moment—impacts others; you literally are contagious. Be worth catching.

Do you choose to positively impact the world by choosing to show up in a positive way? Do you choose to make someone's day? Do you choose to spread the plague of negativity or plant the seeds of joy in others?

BE THE PERSON

Social Excellence is a choice. Social Excellence comes to life through every-day behaviors. Social Excellence hinges upon you choosing to be the person you want to be in every moment. It is through the little choices we make every moment that we build a lifestyle of Social Excellence.

Below are 100 phrases that exude Social Excellence. Many of these were created by Twitter followers (Hashtag: #BeThePerson & #SocialExcellence) and Facebook friends. Zach Hartley, a college student at Ball State University in Indiana, even started a movement to improve the social climate of his campus around the small, momentary choices listed below. These phrases represent simple opportunities that are available in each of our lives every day to live a life of Social Excellence. Which of these phrases inspire you to be the person you want to be today?

Underline, star, circle, or highlight the phrases that resonate most with you.

1. Be the person in a drive-thru who buys lunch for the car behind you.

2. Be the person who doesn't assume everything is okay and stops to ask if there's any way you can help.

3. Be the person who forgoes their daily latte to sponsor a family's presents during the holidays.

4. Be the person who gives the other half of your sandwich to the guy at the intersection that is asking for food.

5. Be the person who lets someone with only one item go in front of you in the grocery line.

6. Be the person who makes eye contact and smiles at strangers—and not because you want to go on a date with them.

7. Be the person who offers assistance to a colleague or classmate that's struggling.

8. Be the person who over-tips on a bill when your waitress is having a bad day.

9. Be the person who picks up the phone to call when a friend's texts make it clear they aren't really "doing fine."

10. Be the person who sends a thank you e-mail/note the next day to your designated driver.

11. Be the person who stops a woman whose skirt is tucked in her pantyhose before she leaves the bathroom.

12. Be the person who stops to help someone after they've just dropped the contents of their purse/wallet on the ground.

13. Be the person who stops to tell someone they have toilet paper dragging from their shoe.

14. Be the person who stops to tell someone they've dropped something.

15. Be the person who takes away the keys from a friend that shouldn't drive.

16. Be the person who walks up and thanks a person in uniform for everything they've sacrificed for you.

17. Be the person who always has great news to share.

18. Be the person who always has room for others.

19. Be the person who anonymously pays the restaurant bill for another table.

20. Be the person who appreciates the little things and shares that joy with others.

21. Be the person who asks a homeless woman to join you for lunch.

22. Be the person who breaks the ice.

23. Be the person who brings a few extra coupons to the store for the friends you'll make in line at the checkout.

24. Be the person who buys two so you can give one to a friend or a stranger.

25. Be the person who cares about important stuff.

26. Be the person who carries a great book.

27. Be the person who challenges the status quo in favor of wild dreams.

28. Be the person who commands attention, not demands attention.

29. Be the person who craves wisdom.

30. Be the person who does what others talk about.

31. Be the person who drinks slowly, eats slowly, and enjoys every taste.

32. Be the person who encourages others to the dance floor.

33. Be the person who exudes exuberance.

34. Be the person who families tell stories of gratitude about around their dinner tables at night.

35. Be the person who freely exchanges contact information.

36. Be the person who gathers people together.

37. Be the person who gets children to giggle on an airplane.

38. Be the person who gives holiday presents from the heart rather than the wallet.

39. Be the person who gives up your seat.

40. Be the person who gives without expecting reciprocation.

41. Be the person who has conversations on elevators.

42. Be the person who has deep, powerful, life-changing conversations.

43. Be the person who hosts every situation.

44. Be the person who is both interesting and interested.

45. Be the person who is constantly looking to make someone's day.

46. Be the person who is the first to volunteer.

47. Be the person who is not afraid to "go there."

48. Be the person who is often asked, "How do you find the time?"

49. Be the person who is often asked, "How do you have so much energy?"

50. Be the person who is often asked, "Where did you learn that?"

51. Be the person who is often asked, "Why are you always smiling?"

52. Be the person who is often told, "I wish I could ____ like you."

53. Be the person who is on time.

54. Be the person who is unique on the inside.

55. Be the person who knows when to say "no."

56. Be the person who listens twice as much as you talk.

57. Be the person who lives a disciplined life with purpose, focused on service to others.

58. Be the person who makes a great first impression.

59. Be the person who makes the first toast.

60. Be the person who makes the smart decision.

61. Be the person who offers a hug when others laugh.

62. Be the person who offers a warm two-handed handshake.

63. Be the person who offers free hugs or high fives.

64. Be the person who others are curious to learn more about.

65. Be the person who others aspire to be.

66. Be the person who others respect and like.

67. Be the person who praises others in public.

68. Be the person who remembers birthdays.

69. Be the person who remembers names.

70. Be the person who returns every voice mail and e-mail.

71. Be the person who says, "How are you doing?" and then waits

for the answer because you care about the response.

72. Be the person who says "I'm sorry" first.

73. Be the person who says "yes" to everyday adventures.

74. Be the person who seeks first to understand, then to be understood.

75. Be the person who shares criticism in private.

76. Be the person who smiles and laughs the most.

77. Be the person who stops the gossip.

78. Be the person who suggests a higher standard.

79. Be the person who tells your mom you love her before you get off the phone. Be the person who does the same for your dad.

80. Be the person who truly wants to learn about people different than you.

81. Be the person who understands her own biases, assumptions, and judgments.

82. Be the person who wakes up first.

83. Be the person who wears a seatbelt and asks passengers to do the same.

84. Be the person who works out while others watch television.

85. Be the person who wraps the gift with a ribbon or bow because the recipient of the gift is worth it.

86. Be the person who writes thank you notes.

87. Be the person whose cell phone scrolls hundreds of names, and every name has been called in the last six months.

88. Be the person who learns to say "thank you" in ten different languages.

89. Be the person who stands up for what's right, not for what's popular.

90. Be the person who notices a friend's new haircut, outfit, or healthy habit.

91. Be the person who keeps things in perspective.

92. Be the person who sings proudly, despite your talent level, when the karaoke machine comes out.

93. Be the person who chooses uplifting language.

94. Be the person who knows she has something to learn from everyone.

95. Be the person who offers a comforting touch.

96. Be the person who puts a quarter in the expired meter of the stranger's car behind you.

97. Be the person who lets the other car merge into your lane.

98. Be the person that takes a friend with him to vote.

99. Be the person who offers to give up the remote control.

100. Be the person who changes the world for the better every day.

Stories of Social Excellence
Danny Thomas

If you walk through the halls of St. Jude Children's Research Hospital in Memphis, Tennessee, you can see concrete evidence of Social Excellence in action. Throughout that miracle-producing building that houses the world's most innovative pediatric cancer research and treatment center for catastrophic childhood diseases, are plaques with names of people who have supported the cause of the hospital. Many of those names, especially from the early years, are friends of one man—Danny Thomas.

St. Jude Children's Research hospital is a treatment center where no child is ever denied treatment because of the family's inability to pay. It treats thousands of young children and desperate families each year. This iconic pediatric medical Mecca is the physical manifestation of Danny Thomas's integrity, dream, and Social Excellence.

The story of St. Jude's beginnings can be best found at www.StJude. org, but the basic version goes like this. In the 1950's, Danny Thomas had become an internationally known film and television star. He had built up a massive network of powerful players in the entertainment industry. Years before, he had made a personal, spiritual commitment after a moving religious experience. When praying to St. Jude Thaddeus, the patron saint of hopeless causes, Danny asked the saint to "help me find my way in life, and I will build you a shrine."

Once he had achieved fame and wealth, he kept that promise, but realized he couldn't do it all on his own. He determined the best shrine to build would be a children's hospital, and that was quite a massive—and expensive—endeavor. He asked his entertainment friends to help and reached out to businessmen he was connected with. He raised funds the old-fashioned way, by criss-crossing the United States by car, hosting benefits, and asking for contributions to his cause. He shook hands. He shared his story and his dream. He built relation-

ships. He engaged co-collaborators. Eventually, he even turned to a culturally-based organization he was engaged with for the last financial boost to make his dream a reality.

Matt Mattson and Jessica Gendron Williams have had the opportunity to visit St. Jude Children's Research Hospital several times when speaking to many of their volunteers about Social Excellence. But Danny Thomas's legacy teaches these lessons better than any workshop could. The plaques that hang throughout the halls of the hospital indicating financial donors might seem to some like a necessary recognition for wealthy people who want accolades, but the reality is that each of these plaques represents a person who was directly touched by Danny Thomas's personal social network.

Even though Danny died in 1991, because he shook hands, had conversations, shared his dream, and changed the world, today's donors to St. Jude can keep his dream alive. Because he shook hands, had conversations, shared his dream, and changed the world, millions of otherwise helpless children are alive because of St. Jude Children's Research Hospital's work.

SECTION 3

Putting Social Excellence to Work

3.1 ALL LEADERSHIP IS SOCIAL

One of the challenges for us in writing this book has been the balancing act of making the book for the individual reader, and yet also about organizations—people gathered together around a purpose. How could we write a book to help organizations grow, but still focus it on the individual reader? Seems like an irresolvable predicament, doesn't it? Perhaps for lesser authors, but not for us. (Ha!)

But just as we discussed toward the beginning of the book in the section titled "Social Excellence is for Individuals and Organizations," you can't be social by yourself.

Our goal is to encourage individuals to lead others—socially. In fact, our bold assertion is that Social Excellence might soon replace the term "leadership." Maybe that's a pipe dream, but we suggest that perhaps "Social Excellence" *should* replace "leadership" as the description term for gathering people together to positively change the world.

The problem with the word "leadership" is that it conjures up images from a day gone by. Perhaps you picture the iconic CEO running a behemoth company. Perhaps you envision the captain of a ship or the commander of a military unit. No longer is our society hierarchically structured like the military or 1950's industrial revolution era corporate America. Today's leaders are found everywhere through the previously unimaginable connections established by the internet and social media. Leading happens everywhere and all the time by regular folks, despite their title or position in the world.

Because of this new social structure—where anyone can lead at any time— the term "leadership" seems almost anachronistic. It seems like it belongs in old board rooms or on the battlefields of WWII and not amongst the powerful grassroots movements of today's society where entire regions of the world are being overthrown by average, everyday citizens. Powerful humanitarian efforts are being organized in war-torn parts of the globe by groups of caring citizens with a common dream. Diseases are being cured, not because the government has declared it a national priority, but because concerned parents have gathered together to start a movement. Wouldn't "Social Excellence" be a more descriptive and instructive term than "leadership" in this environment? Being excellent within a social world full of brilliant, connected, able citizens seems much more valuable than being able to lead obedient followers.

Like we said, you can't lead nobody. To lead with distinction requires Social Excellence. Preparing people to become leaders without preparing them to exemplify the definition of Social Excellence seems to shortchange the people who are waiting to be led.

Social Excellence as a leadership framework is inclusive, service-oriented, purpose-driven, and most importantly, about human-to-human, heart-to-heart connections that form the bonds of organizations. Put simply, one's ability to lead is determined by one's ability to connect with others.

3.2 SOCIAL EXCELLENCE APPLIED TO ORGANIZATIONS

We have provided instruction for you, the individual reader, to explore and find your most Socially Excellent self. Extrapolating from there, if all the members of any organizations of which you're a part adopt this philosophy individually, it is logical to assume you'd end up with a Socially Excellent organization.

True.

However, Social Excellence might be even more powerful when considered beyond just the individual level. When applied directly to an organization as a whole, Social Excellence can take on a whole new meaning.

Think about an organization of which you're a part and consider these questions...

- Would your organization be better if it were more curious, generous, authentic, or vulnerable with its stakeholders?

- To what extent does your organization demonstrate a belief in limitless possibility?

- Does your organization have a strategy that focuses on its social abilities, network, and impact?

- How often does your organization serve as a host within its greater community?

- Does your organization help its members become more socially engaged or does it keep its members focused internally?

- Does your organization communicate with the outside world out of generosity or selfish intentions?

- When your organization seeks to attract more members, participants, or fans, does it start by talking to strangers about the benefits of joining, or does it start by talking with its already established network of relationships about how they can work together to improve the world?

- How well does your organization listen? Ask powerful questions? Tell compelling stories? Care about the people it interacts with?

Think about all the members, participants, and fans associated with your organization. Imagine them standing in a circle, holding hands. Which way are they facing? Inward or outward? Organizations that adopt Social Excellence will imagine their members standing in that circle facing outward, toward the rest of the world, because they understand that their group is formed to make the world better, not just make its members better. Its purpose, effort, and function become outwardly focused on the impact it can make on the world, not on the amusement of its members.

Perhaps you have seen a local church, civic lodge, or niche club become so inwardly focused that they feel stuck in a downward spiral of decreasing membership and waning impact on the world around them. All the while, organizations of similar structure and purpose in the same community are booming thanks to the passionate, external service of the growing membership.

Social Excellence is an operational foundation for high-performing organizations. Social Excellence is a framework for how an organization chooses to interact with its members, audiences, partners, customers, and community. Social Excellence is more than just a way for an individual to find meaning in their life; it is a values system to help entire organizations become relevant and significant to the world around them.

3.3 THE SOCIAL EXCELLENCE JOURNEY

By now, you understand that Social Excellence is about more than the ability to make friends, although that is a vital component. Social Excellence is a vehicle for meaningful societal change that starts with an individual making momentary choices of connection, continues through the gathering of people together around a purpose of shared importance, and results in a positive change in the world.

Like the far-reaching ripples of a simple pebble splashing into a pond, the progression of Social Excellence empowers a simple individual with the knowledge, skills, and attitude to truly matter to their world.

The Social Excellence Journey outlines the path a person can experience as they apply the principles to their life. The Journey also provides a means of assessing an individual's or group's level of Social Excellence. A person—and eventually a group of people—must fulfill each step in order to effectively progress to the next, ultimately culminating in an individual and their community of influence, deeply mattering to the world in which they exist.

On which step of the Journey do you need to focus? On which step of the Journey does your organization need to focus?

This section of the book will look at all eleven steps on the Social Excellence Journey. The table on page 189 is broken into three columns.

The first column provides the name of the steps in progression from first to last, or top to bottom.

The middle column asks the primary question that must be answered in order to move on to the next step.

The third column provides a short-hand guide for that step from just you—individual steps—to you and someone else—partner steps—to you and all your someone else's—keystone step—to you and your organization(s)—

community steps—to you and your organization(s) as it relates to the greater society—world steps.

STEP	KEY QUESTION	WHO?
DESIRE	Do you understand the value of being social?	YOU
GUMPTION	Do you have the courage to be social?	YOU
COMMUNICATION	Do you have the skills and abilities to interact with people?	YOU + 1
CONNECTION	Can you find commonality with others?	YOU + 1
RELATION	Do you care about the people with whom you interact?	YOU + 1
NETWORKING	Do you track and connect your relationships?	(YOU + 1) + (YOU + 1) + (YOU + 1)...
ASSOCIATION	Do you consider yourself associated with communities or organizations?	YOU + COMMUNITY
ENGAGEMENT	Do you care about and participate in the organizations of which you are a part?	YOU + COMMUNITY
INFLUENCE	Can you change minds in your organizations?	YOU + COMMUNITY
SOCIETAL RELEVANCE	Do you really matter to your world?	YOU + COMMUNITY + SOCIETY
SOCIETAL SIGNIFICANCE	To what extent do you matter to your world?	YOU + COMMUNITY + SOCIETY

Desire
Do you understand the value of being social?

The first step in the Social Excellence Journey recognizes that in order to even begin the path toward the deepest levels of Social Excellence, a person must actually understand the benefits of being social.

Recently, a personal interaction with a scientist on an airplane reminded us that there are plenty of people who truly do not *want* to be social.

A conversation with a seat mate turned heated when he adamantly disagreed with the concept of Social Excellence. He cited that "forcing people to engage with others when they fundamentally don't want to" was wrong (as though that is what Social Excellence is about). He argued that people should be allowed to be alone if they wanted to. While his argument was infuriating on many levels, after clarity and reflection, we actually agree. The quest to pursuing the Social Excellence Journey begins with your own, personal desire.

Desire is one of the personal steps that are internally and individually focused. Desire is about *you*.

Social Excellence begins with desire. A person must have a clear connection to *why* being social will benefit their lives—a desire to be social.

GUMPTION

Do you have the courage to be social?

Many people want to connect with others, but they lack the courage, the bravery, the gumption, the—pardon the phrase—cojones to take the first step toward connecting with others. Actual social anxiety disorders aside, many people allow fear to get in the way of their social potential.

When our Phired Up team engages in efforts to coach people toward Social Excellence, this is often the step on which we spend considerable time. We have found many people gifted with a natural capacity for social connection, but the fear of rejection or embarrassment holds them back from approaching a stranger, making a phone call, or asking a powerful question that could eventually result in the connection they are looking for.

Gumption is another of the personal steps that is internally and individually focused. Gumption is about *you*.

To start the journey toward Social Excellence, a person needs the desire and the gumption to be social.

COMMUNICATION
Do you have the skills and abilities to interact with people?

The next step on the Social Excellence Journey tests an individual's communication skills and capabilities. Smiling, eye-contact, handshaking, remembering names, asking questions, listening, articulating, conversing, being graceful, and using etiquette are all a part of this step in the Journey.

This is the step in the Journey that most people, when first hearing of the Social Excellence concept, assume Social Excellence is all about. Social Excellence does, in fact, require these social skills and abilities, but it is about so much more than just having the capacity for communication.

Communication is one of the partner steps which are demonstrated through one-on-one or group interactions. Communication is about you in addition to at least one other person.

Having the ability to effectively interact and communicate with others is a vital step in the Social Excellence Journey. Mastering communication takes one thing: practice. Some experts have suggested that a skill can be mastered if given 10,000 hours of deep practice. That's a lot. Good thing there are so many strangers in the world... but not for long.

CONNECTION
Can you find commonality with others?

Being able to communicate is one thing, but being able to connect with someone through commonalities and shared experiences or interests is quite another. Living a Socially Excellent lifestyle means seeking connection with other human beings at every opportunity.

Imagine invisible wires connecting the hearts of people. These wires are built through effective communication and are made of the fabric of shared experiences. Being able to find ways to build these connections with a diverse array of individuals is an advanced Social Excellence skill set. It requires powerful questions, authenticity, and vulnerability.

Brene Brown, Ph.D., a social work professor at the University of Houston and researcher focused on the connections built between humans, said in a TED talk,[14] "Connection is why we're here. It is what gives purpose and meaning to our lives." She goes on to discuss how humans are wired to connect neuro-biologically. Interestingly, she also argues passionately for more vulnerability in our lives. She says in that same talk that, "In order for connection to happen, we have to allow ourselves to be seen— really seen."

Communication is one of the partner steps which are demonstrated through one-on-one or small group interactions.

Connection happens when we find shared experiences, passions, stories, hobbies, interests, challenges, or joys with others. Being able to consistently find those connections in anyone, anywhere, is an important step on this journey of Social Excellence.

RELATION

Do you care about the people with whom you interact?

Communicating with and finding commonality with another person represents a powerful advancement on the Social Excellence Journey. Meaningful relationships are built not just on the tactics and techniques of a good
communicator, but on the emotional engagement of people who care about
one another.

Do you care? That is a question that is far too often left unasked. How often do you plod through a conversation with someone for either solely your
own purposes or simply because the conversation is thrust upon you? On
the other hand, how often do you actually pause to emotionally engage in
the conversation and find the reason this person matters to you?

One might actually argue that the Relation step of the journey is reach-
able without the Communication rung. In other words, people could build
adequate connections even if they don't have strong communication skills.
Remember, though, we're not talking about adequate or average—we're
shooting for excellence. As a person progresses through the journey, they'll
find that building meaningful relationships based on caring and shared experiences is far easier to attain if they have those communication skills and
abilities found in the two steps prior.

Relation is the last of the partner steps, which are demonstrated through
one-on-one or small group interactions. Relation happens when you authentically care about people.

NETWORKING

Do you track and connect your relationships?

Networking is the keystone of the Social Excellence Journey. This step transitions the meaning of Social Excellence from being about an individual's capacity to relate with other individuals, to being about building organizations and maximizing a person's impact on their world.

Networking, simplified, looks like you connecting your relationships with each other, on purpose—introducing and facilitating the relationships of the people you care about. Networking looks like tracking who you know, capturing information about those relationships, actually managing your database of relationships consistently (think about an elaborate personal directory that is constantly updated), and generously serving your network by connecting individuals in mutually beneficial ways.

Your network is made of everyone you know.

The concept of a personal or professional network is not new; nor is the term "networking." Within the context of our message, however, networking looks like the scientific application of the art that is Social Excellence.

When working with cause-based organizations that want to change the world, we teach a method of attracting members, donors, and raving fans that is the system, the process, the science that complements the art of Social Excellence. That method—that science of organizational growth—is this networking step done with intention, purpose, and precision. Social Excellence is the art of organizational growth that ensures that the networking is done with pure, altruistic, generous intentions. Put the art and science together and you have everything you need to build a successful community or organization that can change the world.

Networking is the keystone step that transitions the Social Excellence meaning from a focus on one, two, or a few people to larger communities and eventually the world.

ASSOCIATION
Do you consider yourself associated with communities or organizations?

The previous step—networking—pushes people to track and connect their relationships in meaningful ways. From amongst that, webs of connections, communities, and organizations arise.

It should be pointed out again that the communities and organizations we are referencing are the groups of people in an individual's network who share a common bond—a common purpose or cause. As we mentioned earlier in the book, we'll simplify these concepts by primarily using the term "organizations." This could be a neighborhood, club, school, trade association, industry, workplace, city, nation, fan base, or a group of people with particular interest in porcelain dolls. There are likely more organizations than there are individuals, and these organizations are the basis for societal change. Go back to that Margaret Mead quote about small groups of committed citizens. These are organizations.

Think of all the organizations—people organized around a mutual purpose—with whom you currently consider yourself associated. Everything from interest-based groups, to organizations based on proximity (neighborhood, town, etc.), to causes you support, to people you share mutual experiences with, to work-centered groups, to fraternal groups, and the list goes on and on. Which of these organizations in your life do you truly consider yourself associated with—intentionally and not just by happenstance? Moving forward on the Social Excellence Journey requires association with organized groups of people.

Association is a community step which looks at an individual's role within a larger group of people. But Social Excellence doesn't stop with simply a personal recognition of association with a group.

Engagement

Do you care about and participate in the organizations of which you are a part?

Being a member of an organization is one thing; caring about and participating in that organization is quite another. Many people happen to be a part of a group or category of individuals, but that particular group doesn't really matter to them.

For instance, how much do you care about being an alumnus of your school? If you are one of the small percentage of alumni that donates money, attends reunions, wears a class ring, and decorates your home with school paraphernalia, you probably care a lot. But there are many school alumni who don't take part in any of that school spirit celebration. They honestly don't really care about that organization of which they are a part.

Social Excellence challenges you to engage in your organizations as much as possible. Socially Excellent individuals make an effort to care about their organizations. In fact, take a moment to consider which organizations you care for in your life...

Organizations I Care About:

To progress further toward Social Excellence and social impact, a person must not only care about their organization, but take part. They must participate, volunteer, work, challenge, and get their hands dirty to make that community successful.

To participate means to step up into a leadership role of some sort. Participation is often done by twenty percent of the organization and as the old principle from Vilfredo Pareto—a great Italian economist—suggests, twenty percent of the community is almost always responsible for eighty percent of the results. In other works by this book's authors, we have called these participating organization members "horses."

True Social Excellence means being a workhorse in the organizations you care about. It's about stepping up in your communities, organizations, and groups to develop and support the growth of your common purpose. It's about taking action with others to change your world.

Engagement is a community step which looks at an individual's role within a larger group of people. It's the step where you not only belong to an organization, but you care about it and participate in it as well.

INFLUENCE
Can you change minds in your organizations?

Influence is the next of the community steps. This step evaluates an individual's level of sway within your organization.

Do people listen to, respect, and respond to your ideas? Have you built the trust and personal connections necessary to have influence and truly be a leader? Can you change minds within your organization and persuade those involved to improve?

The "engagement" step is about doing the work of an organization and, at most, managing the work of an organization. Influence, as a step in the journey, however, is about leadership—being able to rally people and change minds within your organization.

Practicing the Social Excellence lifestyle every day provides a path for building this influence, not through force or corruption, but through genuine relationship building, modeling excellence, and earning trust from your community.

Influence is a community step which looks at an individual's role within a larger group of people. It's the step where not only are you taking action within the organization, but you have the ability to lead others in action.

SOCIETAL RELEVANCE
Does your organization matter to society?

The final two steps in the Social Excellence Journey are the steps that allow many people to find the deep level of fulfillment they are seeking in life. People want to matter. These two world steps are the levels of Social Excellence that are attained through a consistent lifestyle of every day choices.

To matter to the world can seem like a pretty big undertaking. You're only one small person amongst billions, after all. However, through the power of organization, we all have a very accessible path to relevance in our worlds. Throughout this journey, you've no doubt noticed a progression from self, to organization, and now to world, and that is the path a person can take to truly matter to their world. Once you have achieved the previous steps of this journey, you'll note that you have gathered together with others, you've engaged in that gathering community/organization, and you have influence over that group. Now, the challenge becomes making the group itself influential to society.

The concept of an organization or community reappears over and over and over throughout this book. From political parties, to home owners associations, to the college chess club, to the guild of on-line gamers, to a union of service workers, to a college sorority, to a support group, to The Red Hat Society, to an NGO building schools in Afghanistan, to a book club, to a local mosque, to a multi-national corporation, and everything in between, this is how most people become relevant to society. This is how we matter to the larger world: through association, organizations and community.

So are you associated with people who, when gathered together, matter to society? There are plenty of organizations that are self-serving, inward-looking, and focus on things that only matter to the participants of those organizations. Those are fine organizations, but this journey pushes you, as an influential leader within that organization, to go further.

There are other organizations that matter to the world around them. The organization itself is meaningful within society, and thus you, as an influential leader, matter. This is societal relevance.

So as a leader of your organization, do you really matter to your world? Does your gathering of people, your group, your organization, your community, matter to the people beyond its own walls? Would the world be dramatically worse off if your organization didn't exist? Do you really matter to the world? Yes or no? This is the test of societal relevance.

SOCIETAL SIGNIFICANCE
To what extent does your organization matter to society?

The final step in the Social Excellence Journey simply takes the previous step to the next level. If you matter to society because of your engagement and influence within your organization, to what extent do you matter?

The question of relevance is a powerful one. Significance, though, allows not just for a yes or no answer, but provides space for true excellence to blossom.

Societal significance is the ultimate level of Social Excellence. A person makes the momentary choices that lead to patterns of behavior, which eventually become a lifestyle of Social Excellence. That person then uses their lifestyle to make a meaningful impact on society by working with others organized around a common purpose. They all feel the illumination of Social Excellence.

Significance is the step that allows us space for the continual pursuit of excellence. It asks the question, "How can I, the cause I am deeply engaged in, and the people who are engaged in it with me, matter more to the world?"

3.4 YOUR PERSONAL SOCIAL SIGNIFICANCE PLAN

This section of the book is provided to help you build your own personalized plan to progress toward Social Excellence. Write in pencil throughout this plan so you can come back and enhance it as you go.

The plan will take you through an honest assessment of your current reality, an identification of your plan to matter in the world, and specific action steps with measurable goals to help you map out and track your progress toward Social Excellence.

Remember, Social Excellence is an aspiration. It is a daily challenge and is meant to inspire continued improvement. It is a target that, because it is always just out of reach, pushes you to be a better version of you every day and in every moment. Social Excellence is something to shoot for throughout your lifetime, not a destination to be reached. The Social Excellence lifestyle is one of constant improvement, unquenchable curiosity, and limitless possibility.

Enjoy the journey.

Step 1: Your Current Location on the Journey

Mark your current place within the Social Excellence Journey by writing today's date in the first column of the table below. On the next page, write about your current reality and what it will take to progress through the journey:

	DESIRE	Do you understand the value of being social?
	GUMPTION	Do you have the courage to be social?
	COMMUNICATION	Do you have the skills and abilities to interact with people?
	CONNECTION	Can you find commonality with others?
	RELATION	Do you care about the people with whom you interact?
	NETWORKING	Do you track and connect your relationships?
	ASSOCIATION	Do you consider yourself associated with communities or organizations?
	INFLUENCE	Can you change minds in your organizations?
	SOCIETAL RELEVANCE	Do you really matter to your world?
	SOCIETAL SIGNIFICANCE	To what extent do you matter to your world?

Your current social reality: Where are you on the journey? Why? What do you need to do to progress on the journey? Did you find that you skipped a step along the way? Where is your organization on the journey? Which of the Five Degrees of Social Excellence do you need to work on (handshakes, conversations, relationships, collaboration, organization)? How significant are you to your community? Your world? How would you describe your social self? What words in the definition of Social Excellence do you want to incorporate more into your life?

Reflecting on these questions, record your thoughts below:

Step 2: Why Social Excellence Matters to You

I believe the world would be better if:

and I'm going to do something about it.

Social Excellence will make my life better in the following ways:

How will I matter to the world when it is all said and done?

My personal values that align closely with the characteristics of a Socially Excellent lifestyle are:

If I adopt Social Excellence as a lifestyle, how will the following areas of my life be affected?

Work/school:

Relationships:

Service:

Mind:

Spiritual:

Body:

Leisure:

Passions:

Self-worth:

Step 3: Your Commitments to Action and Goals

Dares: Go back through the book to all the dares you've been given so far. Check out the section on the *Social Excellence Dare Cards* in the last part of this book. And be sure to note the *Ultimate Dare* on page 220. Go through those dares and put dates next to each of them, indicating your commitment to fulfilling them.

Handshakes: Currently, I average _____ handshakes with new people per week. Because every time I genuinely shake someone's hand, it provides an opportunity to connect, to learn, and to influence, I will commit to shaking _____ hands per week. (reference page 130 to measure them over twenty-one days)

Not all handshakes are random. Many are well planned. These are the five people I need to shake hands with who can have the greatest impact on my cause/purpose/organization/world:

1. _____

2. _____

3. _____

4. _____

5. _____

Conversations: My ability to create casual, good, and especially *powerful conversations* can greatly impact my potential to create the world I envision. I will use the four pillars of Social Excellence to improve my conversations with strangers, friends, family members, co-workers, children—everyone. Here's how:

Curiosity: I will use curiosity to improve my conversations in the following ways:

Generosity: I will use generosity to improve my conversations in the following ways:

Authenticity: I will use authenticity to improve my conversations in the following ways:

Vulnerability: I will use vulnerability to improve my conversations in the following ways:

Circle at least fifteen questions in the "One Hundred Questions" section of the book starting on page 229 that can help make your conversations more interesting, more fun, deeper, and more powerful.

Relationships: The people in my personal network deserve my attention and nurturing. The healthier my relationships are, the more potential I have to enlist my network in changing the world with me.

I commit to making _____ calls/e-mails/texts of generosity weekly to help people in my network.

I commit to going to coffee/breakfast/lunch/dinner with _____ people within my network each week to create powerful conversations.

I commit to helping _____ people in my network each week with projects they care deeply about.

I commit to connecting _____ people in my network with other people in my network each week.

This is how I'm going to get started:

Collaboration: Relationships + Actions are the ingredients of world changing movements. What will you do with the people you're connected with? What will you work on together?

I have an interest in making measurable, positive change happen in the world through action. Here are five tasks, jobs, projects, challenges, problems, or opportunities I'm going start working on this month. I will meet up with one of the people in my network to start working on each of these this month.

	Project	Person
1.	_____	_____
2.	_____	_____
3.	_____	_____
4.	_____	_____
5.	_____	_____
6.	_____	_____

Organization: The current organizations I'm connected to or the future organizations I want to connect with that will help me make the greatest impact on the world are:

The Question of Significance: How can I, the cause I am deeply engaged in, and the people who are engaged in it with me, matter more to the world?

How can I matter more to the world?

How can my organization(s) matter more to the world?

Now think bigger than you just gave yourself permission to think. What does a grander vision of your organization's potential look like?

3.5 THE ULTIMATE DARE

WARNING! This is the ultimate dare you should only take once you've read and internalized this whole book. Only turn this page to see the ULTIMATE DARE once you're ready.

WE DARE YOU
(THE ULTIMATE DARE)

Be Generous. Go meet someone new. Engage them in a powerful conversation about how they want to change the world. Share a little about your vision for changing the world. **Give this book to your new friend** as a gift to inspire them to change the world through Social Excellence.

WE DARE YOU.

"But wait!" you might be thinking. "This book has my personal notes, plan, and deeply personal thoughts written throughout its pages!"

Exactly. After a few days, trade them a clean, new copy in exchange for returning your personal copy of the book. When you make the handoff, imagine how much this person will already know about your social aspirations.

Repeat the "ultimate dare" often.

SECTION 4

ADDITIONAL RESOURCES

4.1 SOCIAL EXCELLENCE DARES & FACILITATION GUIDE

"We dare you." That theme has run throughout this book. Many readers will interpret each element of Social Excellence as a personal challenge that dares them to connect with the best version of themselves. Those who choose to accept the dare of Social Excellence will experience the magic of this lifestyle.

Phired Up offers an additional product that serves as an interactive, portable compliment to this book in the form of *Social Excellence Dare Cards*. These business-card-sized resources are available for purchase at www. PhiredUp.com. They provide a pocket-sized tool to learn and teach Social Excellence through small challenges.

The following is a selection of dares from those cards, followed by a guide to facilitate group learning using these cards. This book, along with those *Social Excellence Dare Cards,* combine to make powerful teaching tools for organizations, groups, businesses, and friends who want to challenge each other to become more Socially Excellent.

These dares, when paired with the dares found throughout the rest of this book, should give you just enough practice in Social Excellence behaviors to push you outside your comfort zone and into whole new levels of understanding Social Excellence.

We dare you to...

DARE CARD #13: Grab your cell phone. Scroll the directory. Who are the two people who would be emotionally difficult to call? This card is your excuse to catch up with a lost friend or mend a broken relationship. At the end of the call, explain to them what prompted you to call and challenge them to do the same thing.

DARE CARD #15: Count the smiles you get for thirty minutes. Wander through areas with a lot of people and try to get as many strangers to smile as you can. Keep a tally. How many smiles can you get in thirty minutes? Bonus: count the number of times you can get someone to thank you.

DARE CARD #19: Ask someone for directions, assistance, or guidance. Be authentic. Transition into conversation. Share something meaningful about yourself. Get contact info.

DARE CARD #24: You have five minutes. Look around. Find a stranger. Get his phone number. Introduce your new friend to three people you know.

DARE CARD #25: Engage in a friendly, but passionate, debate. Find a stranger. Ask her about world events, a hot button topic, her most controversial opinion, or anything that will spark healthy debate. Let her know you're just trying to learn something from someone today. Get passionate about the topic!

DARE CARD #33: Be curious about something someone is holding or reading. Offer to help that person. Make his day better. Make his life better.

DARE CARD #47: Rock, Paper, Scissors! Quickly find a small group of people. Challenge someone in the group to a game of RPS. Get the group to challenge other strangers. Spread the fun.

DARE CARD #55: Find someone you're curious about. Without seeming creepy, talk only in questions. Ask her at least ten questions, and then feel free to use statements again. Don't scare her away.

DARE CARD #64: (The "FUTURE" Dare) Find a stranger nearby. Initiate an unforced handshake. Learn his full name and origin. Get him to tell you what his plans are for the next few hours, days, months. Bonus: See if he'll share his life's ambition or dreams with you.

DARE CARD #65: (The "Friends/Family" Dare) Find a stranger nearby. Initiate an unforced handshake. Learn her full name. Get her to tell you about her favorite family members and/or closest friends. Bonus: See if you can identify a mutual friend.

DARE CARD #66: (The "From" Dare) Find a stranger nearby. Initiate an unforced handshake. Learn his last name. See if you can comfortably get him to tell you a story about the place where he grew up.

DARE CARD #67: (The "Favorites" Dare) Find a stranger nearby. Initiate an unforced handshake. Learn her full name. Get her to tell you a story about her hobbies or favorite activities.

DARE CARD #68: (The "fun" Dare) Find a stranger nearby. Initiate an unforced handshake. Learn his middle name. Get him to tell you what he does for fun. *Bonus:* Get him to teach you or demonstrate. Exchange contact information.

DARE CARD #71: Be generous to three people. Help them carry something, give them a gift, make their day, their week, or their month. Ask them to "pass it on" and be sure to get their names and phone numbers. Bonus: Learn about their favorite charitable cause and ask them to teach you more about it over coffee next week.

DARE CARD #72: Look around. Find a stranger who is smiling or exuding positive energy. Let her know you noticed her. Ask her why her day is going so well. Thank her for making your day a little better.

DARE CARD #73: Look around. Find a stranger with a frown on his face. Let him know you noticed him. Offer a compliment or quick story. Can you get him to smile? Laugh? Engage in a conversation?

DARE CARD #79: Compliment two people. Engage them in a sit-down conversation. Learn about their deepest passion in life. Exchange contact info.

DARE CARD #89: Go to Facebook. Find five Facebook friends you haven't met in person or you haven't connected with on a personal level. Ask them to join you for lunch within the next seven days. Ask them to bring a friend so you can build your personal network, not just your on-line network.

DARE CARD #98: Start a dance party. Seriously. Go somewhere with a lot of people. Do what you have to do to get several sober strangers dancing, smiling, and having a great time. Introduce yourself to the people who are most into it. Get their phone number for future dance parties.

DARE CARD #00 (DOUBLE DARE): Find a small group of people. Engage them. Learn what they care about. Start a tribe. Inspire your small group and others to take action on a real issue of shared interest. Change your world in some small or large way. Within twenty-four hours. Go.

Questions for Discussion – *Social Excellence Dare Cards*

After challenging learners to accomplish several dares, engage in a discussion to solidify the learning. Try discussing the following questions:

- On a scale between Socially Excellent and Socially Awkward, where do you currently fall? What has contributed to your current level of social aptitude?

- What elements of Social Excellence are most important for you personally to develop?

- Who are the people in your life that already live a Socially Excellent lifestyle? Can you provide examples of how they do that?

- How could Social Excellence improve your life personally? How could it improve your organization?

- What was difficult to complete the dares? What was easy? What did you learn about yourself by taking the dares? What did you learn about others?

- How can you incorporate Social Excellence and the lessons learned from these dares into your everyday life?

- Which lessons do you wish you had learned just a few years ago? Which do you think you'll need most a few years from now?

4.2 One Hundred Questions

The following pages provide a list of one hundred questions that can help with Socially Excellent behaviors and lead to Powerful Conversations. The list is divided into three sections: Conversation Starters, Fun Zone Questions, and Deep Zone Questions.

Conversation Starters

1. What's your story?

2. How's your day been so far?

3. This is great, don't you think?

4. Am I in the right place?

5. Do you understand this stuff?

6. Can I help you with that?

7. Do we know each other?

8. Are you as excited about this as I am?

9. Did you see that show last night?

10. What's the deal with that?

11. Would you mind if I borrowed that for a second?

12. Do you have any recommendations for fun things to do around here?

13. Do you mind if I sit here?

14. Is it really this time of year already?

15. Would it be okay if I complimented you on something?

16. Could you help me with something really quickly?

17. Could I get your opinion?

18. Doesn't the host look great tonight?

19. Where did you get that _____ [physical item/ accessory]?

20. Do you mind if I wait here next to you?

21. Would you help me and my friend settle a bet?

22. Do you know what time the game is tomorrow?

23. Is this your first time here?

24. Do you know what time it is?

25. What's going on tonight around here?

26. How do you know _____ [host's name]?

27. What's your name?

28. How far is _____ from here?

29. Where would we know each other from?

30. Did you see the news this morning?

31. How did you get here?

32. Are you in charge of this?

33. Would you mind if I joined you?

Fun Zone Questions

34. If you could marry a cartoon character, which one would it be?

35. What do you think are the three best musical acts of all time?

36. What celebrity do you most want to punch in the face?

37. If you could spend a night out with any celebrity, who would it be?

38. Which one country would you relocate to if you had the opportunity?

39. How often do you go over the speed limit?

40. What's your favorite dance move?

41. Do you like to sing in the shower? What do you sing?

42. What do you do when you think no one is looking?

43. If you could be any athlete, who would you be?

44. What did you get in trouble for when you were a kid?

45. What was the most embarrassing thing that ever happened to you?

46. What really gives you the creeps?

47. Who was your superhero when you were a kid? How about now?

48. Do you have any embarrassing guilty pleasures?

49. When was the last time you laughed so hard your stomach hurt?

50. Do you have a signature catch-phrase? If not, what would it be if you had one?

51. Who was your favorite musical group when you were in middle school?

52. If you were to start your own restaurant, what would it be called? What would you serve?

53. Did you go through an awkward stage as a kid? Any good stories from back then?

54. Which household object would you turn yourself into if you had to pick one?

55. What did you do for your most memorable birthday and what age was it?

56. Where did you go or where would you go for your honeymoon?

57. If you won the lottery what would you change about your life?

58. If your life was a TV show, what would the main story line be? What would be the supporting roles? Leading actor/actress?

59. If you were debating soaps/body-washes, would you choose by color or scent?

60. What is your favorite board game?

61. What was your worst date like?

62. If you had to only eat three things for the rest of your life, day in and day out, what would they be?

63. Do you prefer a stormy night with cuddling or a romantic dinner at a nice restaurant with ambiance?

64. What was your first job? Worst job?

65. What was your favorite toy as a child?

66. What is your number one public restroom pet peeve?

DEEP ZONE QUESTIONS

67. What do you bring most to a friendship?

68. Who is the first person you think about when you wake up?

69. When, if ever, do you think it's okay to tell a lie?

70. If you were going to be stuck on a deserted island, which three books/movies/people/foods would you take along?

71. What was the happiest moment of your life? The saddest?

72. Who is the most important person in your life? Would you tell me about him or her?

73. Who has been the biggest influence on your life? What lessons did they teach you?

74. Who has been the kindest to you in your life?

75. What are you really about?

76. How has your life been different than what you'd imagined?

77. Do you have any regrets?

78. What's just below your surface that you never let escape?

79. How do you think you'll matter to this world, when it's all said and done?

80. How would you describe me? How would you describe yourself?

81. What does the "best version of you" really look like?

82. What in your life fulfills you?

83. What is one vivid memory from your childhood?

84. What is the most important quality you look for in a life partner?

85. If you were forced or decided to go one year without phone calls—neither receiving nor making—who would be the last two people you'd call?

86. If you had to verbalize a slogan for your life, what would it be?

87. What are your best memories of grade school/high school/college/grad-uate school? Worst memories?

88. What lessons have you learned from your relationships?

89. What traditions have been passed down in your family?

90. What is the most beautiful image/place/thing you have ever seen? Why?

91. The world is going to end in one hour. How are you going to spend that hour?

92. Have you ever caved in to peer pressure? If so, what was it and how would you have changed it if you could go back?

93. If you could tell your best friend one thing you can't stand about her what would it be? How would she react?

94. What's the nicest thing anyone has ever said to you?

95. What is your most prized possession?

96. What is your crowning achievement at this point in life?

97. What's the best gift you've ever given someone?

98. What is the last movie that made you cry?

99. Has money played a role in shaping who you've become?

100. If most people agreed with you politically, how would the country/world be different?

4.3 ABOUT PHIRED UP PRODUCTIONS

Phired Up Productions is an education firm founded in 2002 that provides membership growth solutions to cause-oriented organizations. Our message is for organizational leaders who desire a higher quantity of higher quality individuals involved in their cause. Phired Up teaches the art (Social Excellence) and science (Dynamic Recruitment) of attracting high quality members to an important cause. The company is driven by a team of innovative, bold, fun, relationship-oriented, values-centered change agents that deliver world-class educational products and services.

PHIRED UP'S REASON FOR BEING

We exist to prepare the world's organizational leaders with the patterns of behavior necessary to consistently increase the quantity of quality people they engage in their cause.

PHIRED UP IS SUCCESSFUL WHEN...

- Membership organizations around the world value and utilize Phired Up's organizational growth system to advance their cause.

- Leaders of membership organizations around the world understand and choose to practice Social Excellence for the benefit of their cause and society.

- Phired Up's values are exemplified in every product, service, and interaction.

- The world is dramatically improved through the work of membership organizations that adopt Phired Up's educational messages and philosophy.

COMPANY VALUES

Social Excellence

Phired Up is committed to teaching, exemplifying, and spreading Social Excellence. Social Excellence is a state of perpetual generosity, curiosity, positivity, and openness to limitless possibility. A desire to intentionally connect with others. The ability to engage in deep, meaningful conversation. Acting in a responsible and respectable manner, with high expectations of others. Being authentic and living everyday with integrity as the best version of yourself. Being confident and vulnerable. Being fun and compassionate. Being open, kind, and bold. The deepest level of societal participation and contribution.

Limitless Possibility

Phired Up is committed to stretching the boundaries of our partners' imagined personal and organizational barriers to performance, and filling in that new space with empowering patterns of behavior. We help organizations move out of their rut of merely acceptable performance and move into the world of limitless possibilities.

Innovation

Phired Up is committed to continual innovation. An organization will never be truly great if it does not continue to innovate. We choose to (and teach organizations to) reject "good enough" at every turn.

The Power of One

Phired Up believes in the power of individuals to revolutionize an organization, a community, and the world. Positive change toward a membership organization's limitless potential is most often the result of one individual. Most of the world's greatest revolutions can be traced to the vision, plan—and most importantly, the hard work—of one committed individual or a small, deeply committed group. We believe everyone has the power to affect positive change, to be a revolutionary, and to change the world.

Focus on the Basics

Phired Up believes that success—no matter the scale—is a result of a primary focus on the basics. Membership organizations are nothing more than a combination of two basic ingredients—people and purpose. Organizational success is only achieved by first concentrating on growing (quantity) and developing the people involved in the organization (quality), in addition to focusing on the exemplification of the organization's purpose.

Systemic, Systematic Performance Improvement

Phired Up is committed to the power of systemic, systematic performance improvement. An organization's performance must always be seen within the systemic context in which it exists. Improving that performance must be done through a systematic, step-by-step process of enhancing knowledge, skills, and attitudes, beginning with building a dream to drive the process.

Pursuit and Dissemination of Wisdom

Phired Up is committed to the continual pursuit and sharing of wisdom. Positive outside influences have the power to alter personal patterns of behavior. Organizations and their leaders should continually pursue knowledge to improve their own lives and society as a whole.

Action

Phired Up is committed to action. Talk is cheap—doing changes the world. We *do*. We teach organizations to do—to execute results-driving actions that advance their cause and improve society.

Relationships

Phired Up is committed to the power of relationships formed through Social Excellence to engage others in a cause. People join people. The quantity and quality of a person's or organization's social network is directly correlated to its potential for success.

4.4 ABOUT THE AUTHORS

Matthew G. Mattson is co-founder and President of Phired Up Productions. Mattson has a B.A. in Advertising and Public Relations and an M.S. in Education. His experience as a member of, a leader in, an educator to, and an advocate for membership organizations is deep and varied. From college fraternities and sororities, to national mental health organizations, to several other not-for-profits, Matt has provided a spark for many groups. He is the proud father of two daughters—thanks to his amazing wife, Meggan— and is an unapologetic Chicago Cubs fan.

Jessica Gendron Williams is a Vice President for Phired Up, and runs the company's Women's Division. She has been with the company since its early years. Gendron Williams has a B.A. in Graphic Design and an M.S. in Education. She is a co-creator of the Social Excellence concept and a deep believer in the power of organizations to change the world. As a young professional, she has established herself as a bold leader—empowering women to gather together around causes important to them and create meaningful legacies. Jessica lives with three manly men: her husband, Ben, and her two dogs, Maximus and Brutus.

Josh Orendi is co-founder and CEO of Phired Up Productions. Orendi has a B.A. in History and Education and a successful background in business networking, non-profit expansion, corporate management, and executive recruitment. Josh has deep interpersonal connections in the Indianapolis area, where he makes his home. His work with cause-based membership organizations has helped thousands of individuals find a way to personally matter to the world. About the only time Josh is not actually shaking hands and conversing with people is when he's riding his vintage motorcycle around the Midwest or enjoying a quiet evening at home with his wife, Denise.

This book has truly been a team project. The whole Phired Up Productions "Phamily" helped to create the Social Excellence lifestyle and this book. In fact, Woody Woodcock can be credited with the concept of a Socially Excellent lifestyle. Vince Fabra created the Fun Zone/Deep Zone concept in his first month of working with the company. Dr. Colleen Coffey-Melchiorre, our in-house research expert, built the Social Excellence Assessment. Matt Geik provided stories and examples from his life and shared with us his amazing ability to meet any celebrity he puts his mind to. Branden Stewart helped to skillfully manage the publication of this tome. And the rest of the team (Doug, Shira, KJ, and Megan) provided amazing feedback, editorial comments, inspiration, and support. The Phired Up team is a demonstration of Social Excellence in action. We are unapologetically changing the world.

Very special thanks, too, to our friend and colleague, Jessica Pettitt. Jessica is a Socially Excellent social justice educator who is changing the world through her own unique, powerful, inspiring way. She provided insight, input, and invaluable editorial assistance with this book and for that we are forever grateful.

Additional gratitude goes out to our pre-publication reviewers: Keith Ferrazzi, Tom Matthews, Mark Frederick, Vivek Surti, Rick Deale, Mike Dilbeck, Kyle Jordan, Lori Hart, Ann Marie Klotz, Sarah Williams, Lisa Goodale, Ellen Shertzer, Ed Lenane, and A-1 Editing Service. Our interior layout designer Caroline Okun and cover designer Lauren Markiewicz added their art to this final product, and made it sparkle. And we can't forget to thank our good friends at Lulu.

Don't worry; we didn't forget to thank… YOU! Our readers are the people who will turn Social Excellence into a worldwide movement—a revolution of kindness, connection, caring, relationships, and excellence. We believe you are the future of the Social Excellence movement.

We'd like to stay connected with you. We'd like to build a relationship with you. We'd like to hear your feedback, connect you with our friends, and share a wealth of resources that may help you along your journey. Here's the best way for us to do that together:

Facebook:	www.Facebook.com/PhiredUp
Twitter:	www.Twitter.com/PhiredUp (don't forget to use the #SocialExcellence and/or #BeThePerson hashtag)
Website:	www.PhiredUp.com
E-Mail:	SocialExcellence@PhiredUp.com
Mail:	Phired Up Productions, LLC
	484 E. Carmel Dr. #335
	Carmel, IN 46032

4.5 REFERENCES & RECOMMENDED READINGS

1. Brooks, David. *The Social Animal.* New York: Random House, 2011.

2. Moeller, Susan, et. al. *A Day Without Media.* Research conducted by ICMPA and students at the Phillip Merrill College of Journalism, University of Maryland, College Park, USA, accessed http://withoutmedia.wordpress.com/ September 16, 2011.

3. Lenhart, Amanda, et. al. Teens and Mobile Phones. Pew Internet and American Life Project, April 20, 2010. http://www.pewinternet.org/Reports/2010/Teens-and-Mobile-Phones.aspx, accessed on September 16, 2011.

4. Smith, Aaron. Americans and their Cell Phones. Pew Internet and American Life Project, August 15, 2011. http://www.pewinternet.org/Reports/2011/Cell-Phones/Section-2.aspx, accessed on September 16, 2011.

5. McPherson, Miller, et. al. Social Isolation in America: Changes in Core Discussion Networks over Two Decades. American Sociological Review 2006 71: 353

6. Maslow, A. H. A Theory of Human Motivation. Psychological Review, Vol 50(4), Jul 1943, 370-396

7. Covey, Stephen. *The 7 Habits of Highly Effective People.* Free Press, 2004 (Revised Edition).

8. Compliment Guys at Purdue University. YouTube video posted March 11, 2009. http://www.youtube.com/watch?v=QShPNcjgtfs accessed on September 16, 2011

9. For all our readers either too young to get this reference or too uncool to watch SNL as religiously as we do, Wikipedia provides explanation: http://en.wikipedia.org/wiki/Stuart_Smalley, accessed on September 16, 2011. Stuart Smalley is a fictional character invented and performed by satirist Al Franken. The character originated on the television show Saturday Night Live, in a mock self-help show called "Daily Affirmation With Stuart Smalley." It first aired on SNL's February 9, 1991 episode.

10. Buettner, Dan. *Thrive: Finding Happiness the Blue Zones Way.* Washington: National Geographic, 2010.

11. Mehrabian, A. Silent messages: Implicit communication of emotions and attitudes. Belmont, CA: Wadsworth (currently distributed by Albert Mehrabian, email: am@kaaj.com). 1981.

12. Hermes, G., et. al. Social isolation dysregulates endocrine and behavioral stress while increasing malignant burden of spontaneous mammary tumors. Proceedings of the National Academy of Sciences of the United States of America, accessed September 16, 2011 from http://www.pnas.org/content/106/52/22393.full.

13. Goleman, Daniel. *Social Intelligence.* New York: Bantam Dell. 2006.

14. Brown, Brene. Brene Brown: The Power of Vulnerability. TEDx video accessed on September 16, 2011 from http://www.ted.com/talks/brene_brown_on_vulnerability.html. Originally filmed July 2010.

RECOMMENDED READINGS

Circle the books you've read and put a star by the five books you would like to read next. If you're willing, we'd love to hear your book recommendations, too. E-mail them to SocialExcellence@PhiredUp.com or find us on Twitter (@PhiredUp) and Facebook (www.Facebook.com/PhiredUp).

The 7 Habits of Highly Effective People
by Stephen Covey

Fierce Conversations and **Fierce Leadership**
by Susan Scott

Never Eat Alone and **Who's Got Your Back**
by Keith Ferrazzi

How to Start a Conversation & Make Friends
by Don Gabor

How to Talk to Anyone
by Leil Lowndes

How to Win Friends and Influence People
by Dale Carnegie

Let My People Go Surfing
by Yvon Chouinard

Little Black Book of Connections and others
by Jeffrey Gitomer

Remember Every Name Every Time
by Benjamin Levy

See You At The Top
by Zig Ziglar

Social Intelligence and **Emotional Intelligence**
by Daniel Goleman

Start with Why
by Simon Sinek

Tell To Win
by Peter Guber

The Fine Art of Small Talk
by Debra Fine

The Four Agreements
by Don Miguel Ruiz

The Gifts of Imperfection
by Brene Brown

The Likeability Factor
by Tim Sanders

The Power of Nice
by Linda Kaplan Thaler and Robin Koval

The Social Animal
by David Brooks

Thrive
by Dan Buettner

Tribes, Purple Cow, Linchpin and others
by Seth Godin

Bowling Alone
by Robert Putnam

Click
by Ori and Rom Brafman

Enchantment
by Guy Kawasaki